THE PRACTICAL ILLUSTRATED GUIDE TO
DOG TRAINING

THE PRACTICAL ILLUSTRATED GUIDE TO
DOG TRAINING

How to train your dog in 330 step-by-step photographs

PATSY PARRY

Photography by Robert and Justine Pickett

LORENZ BOOKS

This edition is published by Lorenz Books
an imprint of Anness Publishing Ltd
Hermes House, 88–89 Blackfriars Road
London SE1 8HA
tel. 020 7401 2077; fax 020 7633 9499

www.lorenzbooks.com; www.annesspublishing.com

If you like the images in this book and would like to investigate
using them for publishing, promotions or advertising, please visit
our website www.practicalpictures.com for more information.

UK distributor: Book Trade Services; tel. 0116 2759086;
fax 0116 2759090; uksales@booktradeservices.com;
exportsales@booktradeservices.com
North American distributor: National Book Network;
tel. 301 459 3366; fax 301 429 5746; www.nbnbooks.com
Australian distributor: Pan Macmillan Australia;
tel. 1300 135 113; fax 1300 135 103;
customer.service@macmillan.com.au
New Zealand distributor: David Bateman Ltd;
tel. (09) 415 7664; fax (09) 415 8892

Publisher: Joanna Lorenz
Senior Editor: Felicity Forster
Photography: Robert and Justine Pickett
Copy Editor: Richard Rosenfeld
Additional text: Rosie Pilbeam
Designer: Nigel Partridge
Proofreading Manager: Lindsay Zamponi
Production Controller: Helen Wang

© Anness Publishing Ltd 2011

ETHICAL TRADING POLICY
At Anness Publishing we believe that business should be
conducted in an ethical and ecologically sustainable way,
with respect for the environment and a proper regard to
the replacement of the natural resources we employ.

As a publisher, we use a lot of wood pulp in high-quality
paper for printing, and that wood commonly comes from
spruce trees. We are therefore currently growing more than
750,000 trees in three Scottish forest plantations: Berrymoss
(130 hectares/320 acres), West Touxhill (125 hectares/
305 acres) and Deveron Forest (75 hectares/185 acres).
The forests we manage contain more than 3.5 times the
number of trees employed each year in making paper for
the books we manufacture.

Because of this ongoing ecological investment programme,
you, as our customer, can have the pleasure and reassurance of
knowing that a tree is being cultivated on your behalf to naturally
replace the materials used to make the book you are holding.

Our forestry programme is run in accordance with the UK
Woodland Assurance Scheme (UKWAS) and will be certified
by the internationally recognized Forest Stewardship Council
(FSC). The FSC is a non-government organization dedicated
to promoting responsible management of the world's forests.
Certification ensures forests are managed in an environmentally
sustainable and socially responsible way. For further information
about this scheme, go to www.annesspublishing.com/trees.

PUBLISHER'S NOTES
Although the advice and information in this book are believed to
be accurate and true at the time of going to press, neither the
authors nor the publisher can accept any legal responsibility or
liability for any errors or omissions that may have been made nor
for any inaccuracies nor for any loss, harm or injury that comes
about from following instructions or advice in this book.

The reader should not regard the recommendations,
ideas and techniques expressed and described in this book
as substitutes for the advice of a qualified vet or dog training
professional. Any use to which the recommendations, ideas and
techniques are put is at the reader's sole discretion and risk.

Contents

Introduction   6

GETTING STARTED   **8**
Responsible dog ownership   10
Consideration to others   12
Children and dogs   14
Neutering, spaying and breeding   16
The effect of breed on training   18
Equipment   20
Feeding and diet   23
Recipes for dog treats   26

TRAINING PRINCIPLES   **28**
Body language   30
Discipline without physical punishment   34
Using rewards effectively   36
Clicker training   38

HOW TO BEGIN   **40**
Bringing your puppy home   42
House-training   44
Handling and grooming   46
Socialization and habituation   48
Puppy classes and puppy parties   50
Play is important   52
Building confidence in the shy dog   54
Teaching your puppy his name   56
Adolescent dogs   58

TRAINING BASIC COMMANDS   **60**
Sit   62
Down   63
Leave it   64
Stay   65
Wait   66
Eye contact   67
Recalling your dog   68
Lead-walking   72
Settle down   74
Retrieve   75
Drop it   76
Phasing out the reward   77
Household manners   78
Sitting when visitors call   79
Distance, duration and distractions   80
Essential training reminders   82

HOW TO SOLVE COMMON PROBLEMS   **84**
Biting   86
Chewing   87
Digging   88
Jumping up   89
Barking   90
Stealing items   91
Stealing food and begging at the table   92
Jumping on the sofa   93
Attention-seeking behaviour   94
Problem behaviour in the older dog   95

Index   96
Acknowledgements   96

Introduction

Puppies learn from the day they are born. Long before they arrive at their new home, they will have learned a great many valuable lessons from their mother, siblings and the breeder. Such lessons include how to get food, play, bark and fight, as well as learning to cope with frustration when the mother stops feeding them and repeatedly walks away. What the puppies learn at this crucial time will help dictate their character, and whether they'll be confident with people and other dogs.

Another crucial aspect of early learning is a puppy's environment. If he is to be sociable and good with

◄ *No breed is too small to learn. The same basic training principles apply to dogs in all their shapes and sizes.*

people, he needs to be raised from the earliest days among people. Regular contact is vital, enabling him to experience the sights and sounds of a busy household. If the puppy is kept isolated in a barn, where he rarely sees his carers, he'll find it relatively difficult at a later stage to adapt to life in a house, and he may be aggressive toward people. The quicker he gets used to people, the better.

The environment in which you live can also have a major effect. If you live in the countryside, it's possible that a dog will be less sociable than his urban counterpart, simply because there are fewer opportunities for socializing with other dogs and people. In contrast, the town dog will probably spend a lot of time in busy parks and walking the pavements to get to the parks, where it's impossible to ignore the scores of dog walkers. The young puppy quickly gets used to a wide range of dog behaviour, from aggression to a friendly hello.

▲ *Dogs need to spend time off lead, getting plenty of fresh air and exercise.*

THE IMPORTANCE OF TRAINING

In addition to these general influences, it's up to you to provide a specific training programme, the first two elements of which involve the food bowl and lead. If you can teach your puppy to wait nicely when you're preparing his dinner, rather than rushing around in a highly excitable frenzy, life will be much easier, as it will be if it he can sit calmly while you

▼ *Mutual understanding goes a long way toward successful training.*

put on his lead. Both lessons will also teach your dog that he'll get what he wants when he behaves well rather than badly.

It's your job to teach your dog in the simplest way possible. Training is a two-way event: you need to understand your dog and he needs to understand you. You need to give unambiguous commands and make sure they are clearly understood. The more black and white your training programme, the quicker and easier it will be for your dog to understand exactly what you want – and the better the results.

REWARD GOOD BEHAVIOUR

Put simply, dogs like rewards. So, if your dog does what you want when instructed, reward him immediately. After several sessions he'll have learned what's required. If he gives an inappropriate response, ignore him. Once he realizes that such behaviour has no benefit, he'll stop doing it.

The onus is on you to make sure you don't reward inappropriate behaviour, because your dog will immediately think that's how you want him to behave. Don't send out the wrong signals. If your dog nudges you to stroke his head and you do so, he

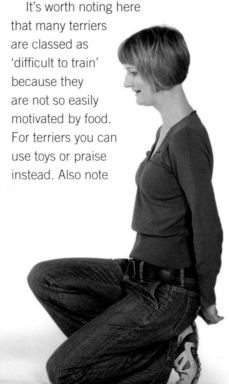

▶ *The bond you share with your dog will be deepened by the training procedure.*

has learned how to get your attention and will do it again. If he manages to steal a tasty morsel from the worktop and is rewarded by eating what he has stolen, he will try it again. If he picks something up and you run after him to get it back, he knows how to get your attention and make you play with him.

Make sure you instil the right behaviour from the beginning. This involves both rewarding the right behaviour and ignoring or interrupting the wrong kind. Get this right and you'll avoid a lot of future problems.

The key to such training is motivation. Motivation has a powerful effect on learning, so it's up to you to work out what best motivates your puppy from the beginning. If he has no interest in treats, toys or petting, then you've got a problem – and a very unusual puppy. All dogs are motivated by something; the secret is finding out what this is.

It's worth noting here that many terriers are classed as 'difficult to train' because they are not so easily motivated by food. For terriers you can use toys or praise instead. Also note

▲ *A well-trained, well-behaved dog will become a wonderful companion.*

that what might seem like a perfectly good motivator to you can actually be a turn-off to your dog.

The best way to respond to any such difficulties is by not thinking of them as 'problems'. Some breeds are easy to train, some are tricky. But the latter are simply different, which means it's up to you to find a creative solution. If you're told that some dogs are stubborn, dominant, lazy or hard to train, don't listen. They've just been trained the wrong way. The problem doesn't necessarily lie with the dog; the owner just needs to take the time to find out what their dog likes.

ABOUT THIS BOOK

This book begins with an overview of responsible dog ownership, and guides you through the processes of welcoming a new puppy into your home. From house-training to playing tug-of-war, all the first steps are explained. There are instructions for training your dog to follow cues, such as 'sit', 'down', 'leave it', 'stay', 'wait' and 'settle down', and also solutions to problems you may encounter. The book aims to make training both easy and fun, and covers all the basic principles a first-time dog owner needs to know.

GETTING STARTED

A great deal of thought and discussion should precede your decision to get a puppy. It is important to choose a breed that will fit in with your lifestyle; for example, it would be foolhardy to acquire a dog that needs an excessive amount of exercise if you lead a sedentary lifestyle. You need to decide if you can put up with the amount of hair some breeds shed; if not, you should look for a non-moulting breed. Whittle down your long list to a few select breeds, and try not to go for looks alone. Ask around vet surgeries and other pet owners to find the best breeder you can. It is also important to take into consideration the costs of your puppy – not just the purchase price, but the cost of vaccinations, health checks, food and equipment. Good puppy classes are an added expense. Owning a dog is not cheap, but well worth the love and affection that you get in return.

◄ *Spending time training your puppy will reap rewards. Home-made treats are a healthy option while training – and you'll know exactly what your dog is eating.*

Responsible dog ownership

Living with a dog is not just a privilege, but also a responsibility that should never be taken lightly. When you first decide to become a dog owner, there are many things to consider. Do you have the time for the dog? Will the breed match your particular lifestyle? Then you need to consider the costs, including training classes, vets' fees (including annual vaccinations), possibly groomers and a high-quality diet. Price is usually the best indicator of food quality; cheap food generally means poor-quality ingredients.

It is also your responsibility to make sure your puppy is good at socializing with other dogs and people, and that he gets regular, daily exercise – even when you don't feel like it because the weather is bad. It is important that your dog isn't a nuisance, either to other dogs or people in parks, or people who live near you. Dogs that have to be left alone shouldn't be allowed to bark constantly and annoy the neighbours, and if they do, it's up to you to find a solution.

In short, make sure you can give your dog all the care and attention he needs. Owning a dog is a long-term financial and emotional commitment.

LEGAL CONSIDERATIONS

In many countries there is breed-specific legislation relating to the ownership of certain types of dog. Most European countries have lists of banned breeds (such as the pit bull, Japanese tosa and Fila Brasileiro), and each state and county of the USA has its own laws. In general, an out-of-control dog is a liability and will be dealt with by law.

It is your responsibility to make sure that your dog is under control, which means training him on a daily basis

▲ *Dogs should never be a nuisance to other dogs or people in the park.*

so that he will come back when called, and won't launch himself at joggers, children and people in the park.

Vaccinations are a legal requirement in most countries, and there are particular laws applying to countries where rabies exists.

Next, your dog needs an engraved identification disc on his collar. This should contain your name and

◄ *Regular vaccinations are a must, to keep your dog healthy throughout his life.*

► *Your dog cannot speak for himself, so an identity disc is a necessity. It should be engraved with your name and address.*

◄ Always carry bags to clean up after your dog. Dispose of the used bags in appropriate bins for dog waste.

the offence. It is always the owner's responsibility to dispose of waste matter. It is not a legal obligation for authorities to provide appropriate bins, although most do. In the UK, councils can refuse to collect household rubbish if it includes dog faeces. Neighbours also have the right to complain to the local authorities if

dog faeces in a nearby garden are causing a smell or health hazard. To deal with the problem, dog waste can be safely composted in the garden, or chemical 'toilets' can be purchased. These look like buckets that are partially buried in the garden and use chemicals to break down solids placed in them.

address, and preferably your telephone number, so that your dog can be returned to you as quickly as possible if he gets lost.

You'll also need to pick up your dog's faeces when on a beach or in the street or park. You might not mind the mess, but other people will, especially those with children. Nothing gives dog owners a bad name quicker than dog faeces left all over the place, dirtying shoes and spreading disease – one very good reason why most beaches are now out of bounds to dog owners in summer.

Furthermore, in many countries – including most of Europe – it is a legal requirement to pick up and safely dispose of your dog's faeces. In some US states it is also an offence for a dog to urinate on or close to a public building. These regulations are enforced by dog wardens or officers employed by the county or state. Penalties vary from a fine to imprisonment, depending on the area fouled and the frequency of

Time requirements

If you are thinking about getting a dog, you should first look at your lifestyle. Consider whether you have the time needed, and whether you are prepared to give it, to ensure a happy human–dog partnership. Some dogs, such as the collie breeds, need a great deal of exercise; others, like some of the toy breeds, do not need so much. All require mental stimulation of some sort. This could take the form of some type of trained activity such as obedience or agility, or simpler

games such as 'find your toy' in the home. Either way, this will take up part of your day – every day for the whole of your dog's life. Dogs also need company and must not just be banished to the garden; you should interact with them regularly. Their every need is your total responsibility. You cannot decide that you are too tired to bother; owning a dog is a life-long commitment.

▼ Regular, daily outdoor exercise makes for a happy dog.

Consideration to others

When you are out and about with your dog, you should always be aware of other dog owners around you, and the effect your dog will have on them. Being a responsible dog owner means consideration to others at all times.

BE THOUGHTFUL

Learn to read the signs. If another dog is friendly and his owner is willing to let him play with your dog for a while, then everything is fine. But if they call their dog back and put him back on the lead, there is usually a good reason. Their dog may have a problem socializing with other dogs or people, and just because yours is friendly toward other dogs, that does not mean you should let him run over while you call out, "he just wants to play". Be thoughtful – put your dog back on the lead before asking if your dog can socialize.

If, however, your dog is the problem, then it is your responsibility to keep him under control at all times. If he is unsafe with people, make sure that he is muzzled, and never – even with a well-behaved dog – let

▲ *Ask first before allowing your dog to socialize with other dogs in the park.*

him loose in the countryside. This is for your dog's safety, the safety of livestock and wildlife, and even your own safety.

DOGS AND LIVESTOCK

The natural instinct of many dogs is to chase and attack sheep, and it pays to remember that sheep do not have to be caught by dogs to be killed. Sheep are 'flight animals', which means they run when they sense danger – possibly straight into a road

and an oncoming car or into barbed wire, where they may die slowly in great pain. They may even run into a stream and drown. Pregnant sheep can be so traumatized by an unfamiliar dog that they may miscarry, causing financial hardship to the farmer.

Many dogs are shot by farmers each year because they have been seen worrying or killing their animals. A farmer is well within his rights to shoot a dog that seems to be a threat, because it is an offence to let a dog disturb or scare sheep, cattle, wildlife or poultry while in the countryside. In the UK, a farmer is allowed by law to destroy any dog that poses a threat to livestock and wildlife. Most European countries also have laws against dogs that chase or kill livestock. In the USA, the livestock law allows farmers to kill dogs that worry livestock; farmers can also charge double the amount it would cost to replace their livestock.

▼ *Keep your dog under control so that he is not a nuisance to other dogs.*

▼ *Taking your dog out and about with you will improve his social skills.*

▲ Well-socialized dogs will be able to play happily together off the lead.

There have also been cases of dog walkers being killed, having been trampled by cattle protecting their calves from out-of-control, yapping, excited dogs. (If you are being chased by cattle, then escape immediately. Do not try to protect your dog; he'll be able to escape much more quickly than you can.)

While on farmland, it's also your responsibility to make sure that your dog does not disturb the wildlife living in the hedgerows. In the UK, a dog must be kept on a lead while on common land and access land between 1st March and 31st July, and all year round on farmland. In the USA, many states require that dogs are kept on a lead at all times except in designated dog parks.

Wherever you walk, always follow simple rules of courtesy. If you go through a gate, make sure you close it properly. Open gates mean that animals can get out and cause harm to themselves or others. Take your litter home with you. The dropped wrapper from your snack could kill if swallowed by an animal. Always keep to footpaths; don't wander through fields of crops. Not only will you damage the plants, but they may have

been sprayed with chemicals harmful to you or your dog. Pick up your dog's waste and take it with you until you can dispose of it correctly. Bags of dog faeces hanging on a hedge do not enhance the countryside. Enjoy your dog walking, but remember that other people and animals have the right to enjoy the great outdoors too.

Respect farm animals
Farm livestock does not just include the commonly seen cattle, pigs and sheep. Deer and game birds are farmed commercially as well. They are naturally shy creatures and you may not see or hear them. If you suspect they are in the area, walk quietly on the designated footpaths. Always keep your dog on a lead. Do not take any risks.

▶ Prevent your dog from worrying horses by keeping him on a lead.

▼ Sheep are wary of predators, so keep your dog well away from them.

Children and dogs

Parents often boast that their children can do whatever they like to their dog, and that he's so good-natured he puts up with almost anything. What such parents often ignore is that this child–dog relationship must be fixed around certain rules.

BASIC GUIDELINES

A child must respect the dog's space and leave him alone when he's sleeping, not pick him up and carry him around like a teddy bear, and never hug him tightly around the neck or kiss him repeatedly, because the dog might respond with a bite to the child's face. In fact, constant cuddling and carrying can easily make your puppy grumpy and snappy, causing owners to think they have an aggressive dog, when really the child is to blame. Remember, not all dogs are keen on close contact. Nor should

a puppy be dressed up like a doll. If that's how a child wants to treat a puppy, then buy them a doll instead. Also make it clear that it's forbidden to pull a dog's ears, tail or nose, and that there's no prodding or poking, even if the dog is blocking the way.

Rewarding children when they are well-behaved with the dog, and vice-versa, will help create a good relationship. Even better, help children to develop a positive relationship with their dog by including them in the dog's training sessions. The dog will learn to take commands from and respect the child.

Young children also need to be taught how their natural exuberance can affect a puppy's behaviour. If a child becomes hyperactive – jumping up and down, shouting, yelling and waving their arms – their dog will also become overexcited, and suddenly

▲ *With supervision, children can take an active role in dog training.*

both are out of control. Worse, the child might hit the puppy when trying to control him. Neither is renowned for patience, especially when tired, so supervise any occasion when children and pets are together.

It goes without saying that a dog, no matter how much you think you can trust him, should never be left alone in a room with a young child. Accidents do happen. Be vigilant outdoors, too, and don't let a young child be responsible for a dog on a walk. Could the child really cope if another dog approached their dog aggressively, and be relied on to pick up the faeces and stop their dog from dashing out into the road? Finally, make sure your child never pats strange dogs. Always get permission from the owners first. Other people's dogs might not be as child-friendly as yours.

GET CHILDREN INVOLVED

Fortunately, it is easy to get children involved in all aspects of the day-to-day care of a dog and his training. Many dog-training classes encourage

▼ *Building a relationship is good for the dog's and children's well-being.*

▲ *If play becomes rough, it is best to move the dog away to a safe place.*

▲ *Ask children to be quiet and leave the dog alone when he is asleep.*

▲ *If there is mutual respect, a good relationship can be built.*

children to attend with their parents, so they can learn how to handle the family dog effectively, and develop a relationship based on mutual respect and trust.

Safety

If you have crawling babies in the home, your dog's food bowl should be picked up as soon as the dog has eaten. Not only might a child try to eat the contents, but the dog may become protective over his food.

However sensible your child is, their friends may not have a good awareness of dogs. Watching both small children and a dog can be an impossible task. On these occasions, it is best to put the dog into another room or in a dog crate. This way neither the child nor the dog will be at risk.

HEALTH ISSUES

A lot has been written about the health risks associated with children handling dogs, but these are actually slight and arguably outweighed by the benefits gained by both child and dog. The main risk is contact with and transmission of round-worm eggs that are passed in the dog's faeces. Worm eggs are tiny and can't be seen with the human eye. However, note that the risk of contamination is far greater when in contact with cats rather than dogs.

Dogs must be wormed regularly with a prescribed wormer, and your vet will advise on how often to do this. Children should be taught to keep their hands away from their faces and to wash their hands after handling their pet, applying the normal rules of commonsense and basic hygiene.

▼ *In time, your dog will learn to respond to what your child asks of him.*

Neutering, spaying and breeding

Being a responsible dog owner means that you will not increase the number of unwanted dogs being sent to rescue centres. Every year, thousands of dogs are put down because they are unwanted, but having your dogs neutered and spayed will stop unwanted pregnancies, and also provide health benefits. Such treatment can substantially lower the risk of prostate problems and testicular cancers in male dogs later in their life, and mammary cancers and pyometra (a life-threatening disease of the womb) in bitches. Neutering and spaying is the responsible, practical approach to dog ownership.

NEUTERING AND SPAYING

It is often thought that castration will cure any problem with an adolescent dog, including jumping up and overexcitement, but in fact castration only helps with problems directly related to testosterone (and definitely

not those caused by attention-seeking). If testosterone levels are high, then roaming the neighbourhood looking for bitches (with the risk of getting run over and causing accidents), scent-marking, mounting inappropriate objects and people, and male-to-male aggression may be remedied, but extra training sessions will also be required. However, contrary to a popular misconception, neutering and spaying does not alter the personality of the dog, nor does it make the dog fat (this is usually caused by a lack of exercise). Both operations will, however, make a dog a more content, happier member of the family.

Spaying bitches will also halt phantom pregnancies, which can

▼ *Veterinary checks of bitches are important to ensure healthy puppies.*

▲ *Bitches can have as many as 12 puppies in a single litter.*

be upsetting for both the bitches and their owners watching them go through this phase. A bitch having a phantom pregnancy may carry a toy around in her mouth as a substitute for a puppy, become aggressive toward other bitches or dogs and become withdrawn and moody, and may stop eating.

People can have strong feelings for and against getting dogs and bitches neutered and spayed, but it's important not to confuse a human's response with what's best for your dog. As for the ideal age, the best advice is to wait until your dog has matured emotionally and physically, although if your male dog is beginning to show behavioural problems caused by high testosterone levels, you should castrate sooner rather than later, before it becomes a permanent problem.

TO BREED OR NOT TO BREED

If you do decide to let a bitch have a litter, it's best to research all the options beforehand. This is a responsible, time-consuming job. Your bitch will

Health checks for different breeds

Even before breeding, it's a busy time. There are health checks for certain breeds of dog: labradors, border collies and golden retrievers are prone to hip problems, and the parents should be hip scored. Hips can only be x-rayed when the dogs are 12 months old. The x-rays are examined by the vet and given a score on nine points of the hip joints. The lower the score, the better the hip joint (a perfect score is 0/0 and the worst is 53/53). Border collies and Tibetan terriers need eye checks; dalmatians are prone to deafness, and cavaliers and boxers are prone to heart problems and need checks before they are mated. In addition, the stud also needs to be checked for potential problems, and both dog and bitch need to have a good temperament with no aggression.

Cavalier

Labrador

Border collie

Boxer

Golden retriever

Dalmatian

need a quiet room away from the hustle and bustle of the house in the first weeks. And if you think you can make a quick profit, nothing could be further from the truth, because breeding is an expensive business.

The first job is to check whether a Caesarean operation is likely, and to make sure you know what to do if there are any problems during whelping. The size of the litter can be anything from 1–12 puppies, with larger dogs producing larger litters – and they all need to be cared for. You will have to start house-training them, oversee the first inoculation, let them socialize and keep them for 8 weeks until they are ready to go to their new homes.

You'll also need to be sufficiently knowledgeable about dogs to impart all the relevant information to the new owners, covering everything from diet and worming to socialization and training – and that's before you have to field their emergency phone calls.

If you do decide to breed from your bitch, check the suitability of prospective new owners by visiting them in their home. Finally, be prepared to take any of the puppies back into your care should anything go wrong along the way.

The effect of breed on training

There is nothing more disheartening than being placed next to a highly responsive border collie or labrador in a training class, which obeys the same command again and again while your terrier is refusing to comply with anything you say, and looks totally, thoroughly bored.

One way around the problem is by being prepared. Knowing the traits of your particular breed means that you should know roughly what behavioural characteristics to expect and what kind of training programme to emphasize.

HERDING DOGS

Collies and shepherds have to be taught to stop herding children and anything else that moves. One way of avoiding this problem is by giving the dog a tennis ball to play with – but use it wisely or he will become so fixated on the ball that he will be high on

▼ *The collie's instinct is to chase, so ball games are good for this breed.*

adrenaline most of the time. If that's all he ever plays with, he'll lose the ability to interact with other dogs.

HUNTING DOGS

Spaniels are hunting dogs and love using their nose to flush out game (labradors are slightly different, retrieving birds and bringing them back to the handler). All spaniel breeds tend to exclude the outside world when they're following a scent, and if yours wasn't well trained to return to a whistle as a puppy, you'll find that no amount of shouting will get him to return. He's not ignoring you; he's just so fixated on the scent that he can't hear you. The advantage of the whistle is that it has just the right pitch to break a dog's concentration.

Similarly, you can get one of the hound groups, for example the beagles and bassets, to come back even though they, too, follow a scent very readily. Again, you must start persistent training when they are young. When

▲ *Huskies have been bred to be fast and to work under harsh conditions.*

training sight hounds such as whippets and lurchers, note that they can be easily bored, so use frequent, brief training sessions lasting 5 minutes.

NORTHERN BREEDS

The Northern breeds – huskies, Alaskan malamutes and Northern Inuits – can also be tricky. All are bred to work independently of their owners, and they can be hard to motivate.

▼ *Because they are bred to catch vermin, terriers excel at digging.*

► *Greyhounds are known for their speed, and are often bred for racing.*

MATCHING TRAINING TO BREED

There are always exceptions to the rule, and your particular dog may actually train like a dream. Toy breeds, such as toy poodles, are intelligent and responsive. So, while each breed trains differently and some breeds have a reputation for stubbornness or being not too bright (bassett hounds are often said to be lacking in brain power, for example), each breed can be trained to a high standard if you make the effort to find out what motivates it and whether the reward you are offering is high on that dog's treat list.

It is also a good idea to check that the reward won't annoy other dog owners who are trying to get their animals to concentrate at the same training session – so avoid noisy toys in a class situation. Squeaky toys may get your dog's attention, but will disturb the whole class. If your dog is easily distracted, make the training sessions short, fun and lively, so that the motivation levels stay high. Terriers, for example, are high-energy, highly active dogs, so avoid slow and tedious sessions for them.

The role of genes

A dog's genes play a significant role in how he behaves and learns: collies are renowned for herding and enjoy working hard; German shepherds are also herding dogs but also make good guard dogs; sight hounds excel at pursuing prey, keeping it in sight and using their great speed to bring it down; labradors insist on retrieving things that you'd rather they didn't; and spaniels love having their nose in the undergrowth, picking up a scent.

Knowing how your dog behaves naturally is vital, because then you'll know what he'll be like to live with. Don't choose a breed if you can't supply its needs. For example, even though you might love the idea of a collie, don't choose this breed if you don't have the time to exercise him.

It is impossible to eradicate a dog's natural behaviour, but with the right training you can steer a dog toward honing his natural instincts to a more manageable level.

◄ *St Bernards were originally bred as working rescue dogs to find travellers lost in the snow.*

► *German shepherds are intelligent and loyal, so they are well suited to working with handlers in army or police roles.*

Equipment

▼ *A flat collar with either a buckle or clip fastening is suitable for training.*

▼ *A body harness has thick straps but may encourage your dog to pull more.*

Pet shops sell a wide array of basic equipment, and it is essential that you have done your homework in advance, knowing the most suitable collars and the best types of lead to buy. Under UK law your dog will need to wear a flat collar with an identification disc containing your name and address, and without these details you could be fined £2,000. Even if your dog has been micro-chipped, he will still need a collar and disc. In many European countries, dogs need to be micro-chipped and/or tattooed. An identification tag is required in the USA, while some states also require that your dog has a licence.

FLAT COLLARS

A flat collar with a buckle or clip fastening is by far the best piece of equipment for training your dog. When your dog is fully grown, buy the best you can afford; a leather collar is the most hard-wearing and is kind on your hands and the dog's neck. Puppies tend to grow quickly, so a cheap collar for them will suffice.

▼ *There is a vast array of basic control equipment on the market, such as flat collars, head collars and body harnesses.*

If you buy a collar with a clip fastening, regularly check that it doesn't become loose and that you can't pull it apart, because if your dog pulls away and the clip fastening comes undone, your dog could end up in the road, causing an accident.

HEAD COLLARS

These are devised to work in the same way as reins on many large animals such as horses, bulls and camels: they steer the animal from the side of the head instead of the strongest part of the body – the neck and shoulders.

There are positive and negative sides to head collars, and they can take some getting used to. It is worth putting one on your dog before giving him a treat, so that he associates it with pleasure, then take it off. Gradually let him get used to it. Some dogs scratch their faces along the floor, trying to get the head collar off, or rub themselves up and down your legs because they do not like the feel of it. The problem is it can be hard for the dog to concentrate on what you want

him to do if he is uncomfortable wearing a head collar. If he keeps pulling on it while being trained, he could end up walking sideways, which can damage his neck.

Head collars are often mistaken for muzzles, and so other dog walkers may give you a wide berth when out walking. On the other hand, a head collar is useful for stopping an aggressive dog from staring at other dogs. If your dog really doesn't like a head collar, then you could consider using a body harness instead.

BODY HARNESSES

There is a wide choice of body harnesses on the market, but choose wisely. The best kinds have a front and back or side attachment, and need a double-ended lead, which means that your dog cannot pull you from his strongest point – his shoulders. The weight is evenly distributed by the lead being attached to the front and side of the harness. The harness stays away from the dog's neck area and won't interfere with his natural body language when approaching another dog. Avoid those with very thin harness straps, because they can chafe

▼ *Retractable leads are popular but a leather lead is better for training.*

▼ *A crate is useful for house-training and for taking your dog in the car.*

under the dog's legs and cause pain and discomfort. Look for wide straps with padding.

Most harnesses are unsuitable for training your dog to stop pulling, and you only have to watch a team of huskies to understand how the harness lets them pull. A fixed harness without the use of a double-ended lead can only encourage your dog to pull, the lead being attached to the back and front of the harness in the middle of the chest.

LEADS

Buy the best you can afford. Once your puppy has got through the chewing stage, buy a good leather lead that is kind on the hands and long-lasting.

Retractable leads are very popular but are not suitable for training, because they can actually encourage dogs to pull, since they allow the animal to go to the end of the lead. In some situations they can be dangerous, with the lead getting tangled around your legs or another dog's feet, which could lead to a fight. Your dog could also run out into the road if you are not quick enough to put on the lock, and the lock mechanism could fail or the lead might snap, resulting in a car

accident. A retractable lead should only be put on your dog when you have arrived at the location where he's going to be walked.

CRATES

A crate is absolutely essential for the puppy owner. It is an invaluable aid to house-training because you can contain your puppy when you cannot watch him – puppies dislike messing the area that they sleep in, and so will cry to be let out to go to the toilet.

A crate also provides a safe place for times when you cannot supervise your dog. It makes a snug sleeping place and a place of safety in the car. (If your car does not fit a dog crate in the back, you should restrain your dog with a harness that attaches to the seat belts.) However, never keep your dog locked up in a crate for hours, and don't

▶ *You can use padded cushions, rugs or plastic baskets for your dog's bedding.*

use it as punishment. Get a crate that's large enough to fit him when he's an adult, and in which he can stand up and move around.

BEDDING

Since puppies and adolescents are prone to chewing and may still have the odd accident, it is best to choose bedding for them that is hard-wearing and easily washable. Plastic dog beds will suit a puppy best, until he is over the chewing stage, and then there is a vast array of beds to choose from. When your dog is an adult, you can use whatever you want for his bedding.

▼ *A basket containing a cushion and a washable fleece makes a comfortable and practical bed.*

▼ *There are many types of food bowls, including stainless steel and ceramic.*

▼ *Match the size of the food bowl you choose to the size of your dog.*

FOOD AND WATER BOWLS

There are many types of bowls on the market. The best are the stainless steel bowls that are hard-wearing and tough. Cheaper plastic bowls should be avoided – they can be easily chewed, and splinters could cut your dog's mouth or be swallowed.

BRUSHES AND COMBS

Even if you have a short-haired dog, it is a good idea to brush him once a week to keep his coat in good condition.

▼ *Groom your dog every week. His coat will benefit, and he will enjoy the attention and get used to being held.*

TREAT BAGS AND WASTE BAGS

Any small bag that can hang around your waist can be used to carry treats. Waste bags should also be carried around at all times. Eco-friendly biodegradable waste bags are now available at most pet stores.

CLICKERS AND WHISTLES

These useful training aids are now available from most pet stores.

▲ *A clicker and whistle, tug toys, squeaky toys and teething toys.*

TOYS

There are more toys on the market for dogs now than there have ever been before. There are tug toys, interactive toys, educational toys, home-alone toys, teething toys, training toys and ball-on-a-rope toys. There are squeaky toys for terriers, fetch toys for retrievers and balls for collies.

One of the best-selling dog toys is the Kong, an interactive stuffable toy that can keep any dog quiet for hours. Stuffing it with some of your dog's daily diet will teach him it is rewarding to be left home alone. It can also be used to reward your dog for being calm when you have visitors, and will keep him busy if he has to be shut in his crate for any amount of time.

It is neither wise nor economical to buy cheap plastic toys, especially for puppies. Cheap toys are easily ripped apart by sharp teeth, and they are usually made of hard plastic which can lodge in the puppy's tummy and cause an expensive trip to the vet.

Feeding and diet

'You are what you eat' applies as much to dogs as to humans. Feeding your dog the best-quality diet will save you money in the long term, with fewer visits to the vet, but trying to make an informed choice about the best diet can be tricky, and no two dog owners agree. While one diet may suit one dog, it may not suit another. The main point is to avoid a poor diet, which can be the root cause of behavioural problems, obesity and poor health. Your dog's overall health and well-being depends on you.

The breeder should have sent you home with some of the food that he or she has been giving your puppy, which has just been weaned off his mother. It is important not to change this diet straight away, because the puppy will already be anxious about leaving his mother, and you don't want to give him stomach problems too.

Fortunately, there are foods specifically designed for puppies (with higher protein content to fuel the puppies' rapid growth rate), juniors, adults, seniors and those with a sensitive stomach. Use the best-quality diet that you can afford, but don't be influenced by colours. Deep, rich colouring is added by the manufacturer to make you buy a particular brand, but your dog will not notice. In the end, all that counts is that your dog is alert and lively, and has a healthy coat.

A dog needs nutrients to provide the energy it needs for running, playing and working. These nutrients consist of protein, fats and carbohydrates.

PROTEIN

This consists of 9–12 amino acids. It is often assumed that the quantity of protein in a dog's diet is the crucial point, but the *quality* of protein is equally or even more important. Protein can come from both animals and plants, but you should check the food label and look for an animal source, ideally chicken, lamb or turkey. Plant proteins (e.g. wheat, corn, soya and rice) are poorer and cheaper.

Dogs that work for a living – for example, police dogs, sheep dogs (dogs that work with farmers, but not border collies), those that work to the gun during the shooting season, search-and-rescue dogs and sniffer dogs – need plenty of protein because they use up so much

Problems due to poor diet
If your dog is getting the wrong diet, he may suffer from some of the following problems:
- Not eating his food
- Wind
- Large volumes of faeces that smell bad
- Teeth coated with tartar
- Heavy scratching or skin infections
- Being overweight with a dull coat
- Being prone to ear infections
- Being touch-sensitive
- Being hyperactive
- Chewing his feet a lot
- Having a poor immune system

Problems due to lack of protein
If you do not provide enough animal protein, then your dog may show one of the following symptoms:
- Poor appetite
- Upset stomach, diarrhoea or vomiting
- Skin problems
- Ear infections
- Hair loss
- Aggression
- Lack of energy
- Shyness

energy during the day. A pet dog does not need as much protein because he'll probably be relatively sedentary, rarely breaking into a sweat.

▼ *Dry food is nutritionally dense and can be easily stored in a cupboard.*

▲ *Wet food has a high moisture content, so more is needed compared to dry food.*

▲ Butcher's scraps – canned or fresh – is not a complete feed.

▲ Canned chicken must be balanced with other additional foods.

▲ Frozen chicken is a cheap way of providing protein for small dogs.

▲ Commercial canned food may be a complete feed or mixed with dry food.

▲ Rice is a source of carbohydrates, suitable for home mixing.

▲ Dry complete feeds have become popular, providing an all-round diet.

▲ Semi-moist feeds must be kept in sealed packets and eaten once open.

▲ The traditional all-round feed of biscuits with gravy is very popular.

▲ Ordinary dry dog biscuits are not adequate as a dog's only food.

▲ Most dogs will eat anything – and because they don't discriminate, they may inadvertently eat something that is not good for them and become ill.

▲ Because dogs can quickly become dehydrated after exercise, a fresh supply of clean drinking water is essential as soon as they get home.

Protein is made up of amino acids, and when wet and dried animal food is heated in the manufacturing process, some of these acids are partially destroyed, thereby reducing the protein levels in the original foodstuffs.

When comparing the protein quantity of a dried food with a wet food, you need to do some calculations to subtract the moisture in the wet food. Wet food has about 75 per cent moisture and dry food about 10 per cent, so the wet food will actually have a higher protein content than dry food, although from the labels you might think it was the other way around.

◀ *Chews satisfy your dog's urge to chew, and will keep his teeth clean.*

Soya is added by some pet food companies as a cheaper protein source, and this may be written on the label as 'derivatives of vegetable origin'. While soya is high in protein, it does interfere with the absorption of other nutrients and can result in damage to the intestinal surface, and create prodigious amounts of wind. It also reduces the digestibility of protein, so your dog will not absorb all the protein that he needs.

FATS

These come in either saturated or polyunsaturated form, and a dog needs both kinds to supply the essential fatty acids to keep him healthy. The difference between the two kinds is that saturated fats come from an animal source and give your dog energy, while polyunsaturated fats come from a vegetable source and generate a healthy skin and coat. Buy a dog food with both added animal and vegetable oils.

CARBOHYDRATES

Dogs need carbohydrates to fuel their energy and mental activity/brain, but they do not need as many carbohydrates as protein, making a diet low in carbohydrates and high in protein ideal. Diets that are rich in carbohydrates take longer to digest and can produce a large number of stools, and your dog will also suffer from wind.

Avoid dog foods where the prime ingredient is grain, e.g. brown rice, oats and barley, because this is basically used as a cheap filler, although grain does contain vitamins, minerals, proteins and fats.

PRESERVATIVES

Most dog foods need preservatives to stop the fats from going rancid. Preservatives, or anti-oxidants, are either natural or artificial. The more natural the preservative, the better it is for the dog, although the shelf-life will be shorter than for foods with artificial preservatives, and the price higher.

There is some debate about safety of the latter, the most controversial anti-oxidant being ethoxyquin, which has been used as a preservative in animal foods for over 30 years, while also often being used as a pesticide. Owners have reported various disadvantages with

their dogs when using food preserved with ethoxyquin, including behavioural and medical-cum-carcinogenic problems. The two other most commonly used artificial preservatives in dog foods are BHA and BHT, again both are thought to be carcinogenic.

The problem is that it's hard to find these preservatives on the label because they're hidden by other terms and words, and sometimes the food companies get around the problem by saying that the contents are preserved with anti-oxidants. The food companies also buy the raw ingredients with these preservatives already added, and state that they have "no added chemicals, preservatives and colours", implying that they have not added anything. They don't need to. Somebody has already done it.

If you want to use dried dog food, look for one that is preserved with natural vitamin E or vitamin C, but the lack of moisture means that you must make sure your dog's water bowl is topped up with fresh water at all times.

▲ *Commercial-bought treats can be high in sugar and additives, such as colouring, and should be avoided or used very sparingly.*

▶ *Sliced carrots and cubes of cheese are a much healthier option.*

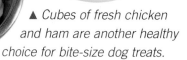

▲ *Cubes of fresh chicken and ham are another healthy choice for bite-size dog treats.*

Recipes for dog treats

The advantage of making home-made treats is that you know exactly what is going into your dog. Shop-bought treats can be high in sugar, over-processed and full of artificial colours, chemicals and preservatives, causing your dog to put on weight, and too many sugars can be detrimental to his behaviour. Home-made treats are a much healthier option, and they are usually a lot more enticing and exciting than anything you can buy from the shop.

Liver cake is an old favourite of many dog trainers, and is very easy to make. On the downside, it doesn't smell very nice and doesn't keep well, so when you make it, cut it into cubes immediately and freeze what you are not going to use.

HOME-MADE DOG BISCUITS
225g (8oz) sausage meat
225g (8oz) wholemeal
(whole-wheat) flour
50–85ml (2–3fl oz) stock
or water

Preheat the oven to 180°C (350°F). Mix the sausage meat and flour with the stock or water to form a scone-like dough. Roll the dough out to 1cm/½in thickness, cut into squares and put on an ungreased baking tray. Bake in the oven for 30–50 minutes, depending on size.

LIVER CAKE
450g (1lb) liver
1 garlic clove
1 egg, beaten
225g (8oz) flour

Preheat the oven to 180°C (350°F). Line a baking tray with baking parchment or grease well. Liquidize the liver, garlic clove and egg. Pour into a bowl and add enough flour to make a scone-like consistency. Pour on to the tray and smooth out. Cook in the oven until you can insert a knife blade and pull it out cleanly. Leave to cool, cut into cubes and freeze whatever you do not use.

LIVER TREATS
450g (1lb) liver
1 garlic clove

Preheat the oven to 150°C (300°F). Bring the liver and garlic to the boil in a little water; simmer for 5 minutes until thoroughly cooked. Drain on kitchen paper and cut into small pieces. Spread on a baking sheet and bake in the oven for half an hour. Turn off the oven and leave until cold. Liver treats do not keep well, so freeze what you are not going to use immediately.

▼ *Some dogs have a big appetite. Regulate food intake to suit activity.*

TUNA BROWNIES

2 x 175g (6oz) cans tuna in water
2 eggs
1 garlic clove, crushed
115–175g (1–1½ cups) wholemeal
  (whole-wheat) flour
Parmesan cheese

Preheat the oven to 180ºC (350ºF).
Liquidize the tuna, eggs and garlic, pour
into a bowl and add enough flour to
make a scone-like consistency. Spread
on to a greased baking tray, or one
lined with greaseproof paper. Sprinkle
with Parmesan cheese. Bake in the
oven for 15 minutes. Cut into small
squares. This recipe freezes well.

CHEESE AND GARLIC BITES

115g (1 cup) flour
115g (1 cup) grated cheese
15ml (1 tbsp) garlic powder
15ml (1 tbsp) margarine, softened
120ml (½ cup) milk

Preheat the oven to 180ºC (350ºF).
Mix the flour and grated cheese,
add the garlic powder and softened
margarine, then slowly add the milk to
form a stiff dough. Knead on a floured
board and roll out to 1cm (½in)
thickness. Cut into shapes and bake
in the oven on an ungreased baking
tray for 15 minutes. Keep in the
refrigerator to maintain freshness.

TUNA TRAINING TREATS

2 x 175g (6oz) cans tuna in water,
  undrained, or sausage meat
2 eggs
1 garlic clove, crushed
115–175g (1–1½ cups) wholemeal
  (whole-wheat) flour

Preheat the oven to 250ºC (480ºF).
Mix the tuna or sausage meat, eggs
and crushed garlic together, adding
the flour gradually until the mixture
has the consistency of a ball of dough.
Flatten the dough out to about 1cm
(½in) thick on a baking sheet. Bake
in the oven for 30 minutes. Cut into
1cm (½in) cubes.

Garlic

Many dogs
are attracted
to garlic – the
bulb of a plant
that is from the lily family –
because of its strong taste and
pungent smell. A few dogs
intensely dislike it, however,
and some people find the smell
unpleasant as it can linger on the
hands. If this is the case, it can
be safely omitted from any of the
treat recipes shown here without
detracting from the finished result.
Find out what your dog likes best.

▲ *Reward your dog with praise and*
a treat when he responds to your cue.

▲ *Use your dog's favourite, extra-tasty*
rewards in distracting environments.

TRAINING PRINCIPLES

Training your dog will be the most important thing that you ever do with him. It builds up a trusting relationship, teaches you how your dog thinks and works, and will significantly improve your dog's behaviour. You should only carry out training when you are both in the mood for fun. If you are in a bad mood or your patience is low, stop immediately. Do the same if the training is going wrong; don't get frustrated with your dog if he does not seem to understand what you want. It's more likely to be your fault for not making your instructions clear. We often talk too much to our dogs, and during training this can cause confusion. That is not to say that you shouldn't talk to your dog, but during training you should keep it to a minimum to avoid causing any distraction. Also make sure that when different members of the household are training your dog, everyone is using the same commands.

◀ *Playing with your dog is an important part of training. It will keep him fit, as well as teaching him to behave well by responding to your cues.*

Body language

Dogs communicate with each other and other species by using body language. If they are happy, sad, uncertain or about to bite, they will immediately communicate it. Being able to read the signals means that you can calm an anxious dog, for example, and avoid situations where he might bite. Being sensitive and alert to what a dog is trying to say also makes for a better relationship.

BODY

The dog uses his body posture to show submission or dominance. If he wants to appear dominant, he will make his body look larger by standing straight-legged and on his toes, with his head held high. In addition, a ridge of hair that runs down the back and lower neck – called the hackles – may stand erect. Some dogs will also put their heads across the back of a dog that they wish to dominate.

Submissive dogs, on the other hand, will do the complete opposite. They try to make themselves look as small as possible by keeping close to the ground and moving in a crouched manner, with their heads held low.

TAIL

There are three key points relating to a dog's tail. First, the tail is a barometer of the dog's emotional state. When looking at the tail, always remember how that particular breed holds it. Some breeds – such as boxers, dobermans and huskies – naturally hold the tail high, which can make it hard for other breeds to read any signals. Now that tail-docking is illegal in many countries (although the USA does still allow tail-docking and ear-cropping), it gives us more scope to read the emotional state of the boxers, dobermans, spaniels and rotweillers that once went tailless.

▲ *Some breeds naturally hold their tail high.*

▲ *Other breeds naturally hold their tail low.*

▼ *A play bow is a signal that your dog wants to start a game.*

▲ *A relaxed tail should be neither erect nor tucked under the body.*

▲ *A full-on body posture can be very intimidating to both dogs and people.*

▲ *A dog rolls over on to his back to show submission to another animal.*

▶ *Terriers love to jump up on their hind legs.*

Second, note the natural position of your dog's tail so that you can read the signals when his emotional state changes. A confident dog will hold his tail high with just the tip giving a slow wag, and this usually happens when a male dog meets another male dog, usually adolescents. A happy, confident dog wags his tail from side to side, a frightened dog has a low tail, and a very scared dog might hold his tail so far between his legs that it may touch his stomach. If your dog's tail wags in a line from the end of the spine, from side to side and slowly, combined with lips pulled back, teeth bared, hackles raised and body stiffness, you are dealing with a state of aggression.

EARS

The position of your dog's ears needs to be read in conjunction with other visual signals. Some dogs hold their ears back and even flat against the head as a greeting gesture or in appeasement. If the ears are held back as a greeting, the mouth will usually be open and the tongue out. A dog that is afraid may have his ears held flat against his head, while a bold, alert dog usually has upright, forward-pointing ears.

▼ *This relaxed, soft-eyed dog appears happy, trusting and confident.*

▲ *An alert, interested dog will have his ears pricked up and pointing forward.*

EYES

In the absence of training, dogs generally do not regard direct eye contact as a pleasant experience; it's actually seen as a threat. In the past, some dog trainers used to give dogs a shake by the scruff and stared them down to make them submissive and comply with an order. But all that this achieved was to make the dogs even more wary of eye contact, possibly resulting in a bite as they defended themselves from further stress. It's therefore important to explain to children, who are at eye height with dogs, that they should not stare directly at their dog.

▼ *This collie's eyes are fixated on any movement, ready to chase an object.*

▲ *A dog that is unsure shows he is tense by holding back his ears.*

With training, however, it is possible to teach dogs eye contact, and this should be done right at the start of your training programme. When taught correctly, dogs can actually find it a rewarding experience, and it can help raise the confidence of a timid animal. It can also speed up the training process because your dog will learn to look you in the eye for further instructions, registering your pleasure when he gets something right.

If a dog is stressed, worried, frightened or overexcited, his pupils may dilate. You should learn to read these signals in conjunction with other aspects of his body language.

▼ *The sideways, cautious look indicates that this dog is wary.*

▲ *With his mouth closed, this dog could be tentative and unsure.*

▲ *Bared teeth indicates an aggressive threat and could result in a bite.*

▲ *A yawn may signal that your dog is rather anxious or worried.*

MOUTH

If your dog has his mouth closed with the sides pulled back, he is rather unsure of himself, while a top lip curled to expose teeth is a warning signal. This remarkably effective threat is often used after more subtle signals have been ignored. If this signal is also ignored, the dog may increase the threat level by curling his lips to expose the major front teeth, with the mouth partly open and the nose area wrinkled. If you ignore that, he'll curl his lips right back, exposing all the major teeth and the gums above the front teeth, with very noticeable wrinkling above the nose. Ignore that, and he'll probably bite.

YAWNING

Sometimes mistaken for boredom, yawning is often displayed when a dog doesn't understand what you want him to do in a training session. If this happens, go back a couple of stages to help him. Yawning may also happen when the dog is in a situation that he cannot cope with – for example, if a child is invading his space.

SMILING

Various breeds, such as terriers, dalmatians and dobermans, are known 'smilers'. Smiling can be a submissive gesture, but it is certainly not aggressive. Most owners find this natural action endearing and charming.

HACKLES

Often misunderstood, hackles can easily be mistaken as an aggressive display. They can be erect in one long line from the base of the neck all the way down to the tail, or just at the neckline. While hackles are a sign of arousal, the source can vary from playing with another dog to approaching a strange dog, usually two adolescent males, or visitors coming into the home.

INTERPRETING THE SIGNALS

You need to be adept at reading several body signals simultaneously. It's no good just reading the tail without seeing what the ears and eyes are doing. For example, if your dog is looking away from you, not making eye contact and possibly licking his lips, he is nervous. You can then ask yourself what has caused his anxiety. Have you inadvertently threatened him? Is your body language making him uneasy? To check what's happening, think about what you are doing at that moment, and try not to repeat it. Note that leaning over your dog can be threatening to a shy animal, and should always be avoided.

◄ *Barking may be either attention-seeking behaviour or just excitement. Once you learn to read your dog's body language, you'll be better able to understand the causes of it.*

One common problem that many dog owners make is in thinking that their dog really does know when he has done something wrong. But that's not necessarily the case. Dogs aren't human, and they don't share our moral code of right and wrong.

If you come home to find that your dog has raided the bin and scattered everything over the floor, for example, you might be tempted to shout at him. He will probably run away and hide. However, this behaviour is a direct response to your threatening body language and aggressive arm movements rather than his earlier bin-raiding behaviour. He is now trying to calm you down and defuse the situation by using body language. He is, in fact, being incredibly sensible. If you start imagining that dogs are human, you'll be very disappointed – which brings us on to stress.

▼ *Dogs will be dogs – there is no point in shouting after the event.*

Sensitivities to stress

Dogs vary in their ability to cope with stress, and the sensitive breeds start suffering more readily than the more robust kind. But also be aware of your own dog's particular personality. Keep an eye out for the following factors, all of which can cause stress:
• Lack of early socialization, making it difficult for your dog to cope with everyday events
• Inappropriate training methods
• Inconsistent treatment of your dog, with different family members sending out conflicting messages
• Showing frustration at your dog's behaviour
• Punishment
• Unrealistic expectations – don't forget, we're talking about a dog!

STRESS

A natural part of our daily lives, stress occurs to some degree whenever we learn anything new. In this respect, dogs are no different from people. Learning will actually be quicker and more effective if there is some degree of stress, provided that it energizes and doesn't badly affect those concerned. (Too much stress for your dog can increase blood pressure and heart rate, and breathing may become panting.)

If you ask your dog to do something he can't mentally cope with, he may become silly, jump up or bark and lunge at other dogs, or he may 'shut down' by lying down and looking bored. If he yawns and scratches when you ask him to do something, you shouldn't conclude that he is bored; he probably just can't cope with what you are asking.

▲ *Dogs can become withdrawn and even ill if they are feeling stressed.*

It's also worth pointing out while on the subject of stress that, in extreme cases, other parts of the dog's body might be affected. The digestive system is usually one of the first things to suffer, causing diarrhoea, or your dog may go off his food or vomit. Others can suffer from excessive coat moult that may only continue for a few hours. Some dogs might self-mutilate or lick walls, and some breeds revert to what is called 'breed-specific behaviour'. For example, collies will round up children, cars or joggers; pointers will point; and labradors will carry items around in their mouth. In other cases, dogs may start chasing shadows or flies. If the immune system is affected, dogs become prone to illness and may get itchy skin or an allergy.

Avoiding stress

Always remember to finish a training session on a good note. If the session is going badly, then the best thing is to finish. It will not have a negative effect on your dog if you just stop and do something else.

Discipline without physical punishment

Unfortunately, physical punishment still plays a part in some people's dog training methods, with equipment such as rattle bottles, check chains, water sprays and spray collars at one extreme, and electric-shock collars at the other. Such devices are designed to cause pain in order to stop a dog from doing something. But not only are they obscene, they also fail to remedy the cause of the dog's behaviour, nor do they communicate to the dog what he should be doing.

NEGATIVE CONSEQUENCES OF PHYSICAL PUNISHMENT

Although you might get some results by smacking a dog when he's unruly, you'll get just as many instances of failure and psychological damage. Punishment always has a consequence, and you have to consider the possible side effects

▼ If you need to punish your dog, calmly say "that's enough" and walk away.

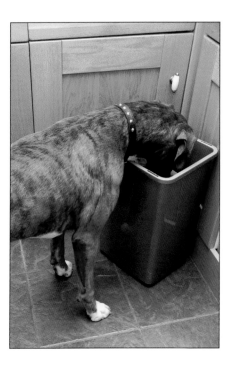

very carefully before striking a dog. Three possible consequences are: relationship problems; more behaviour problems; and subdued behaviour because the dog is too scared to behave in any other way in case he is punished for it.

One form of punishment that has persisted over the years is rubbing a dog's nose in the offending mess when he uses the house as a lavatory. But this simply tells the dog that his owner is not to be trusted, and that making a mess in front of him means trouble. This makes house-training even harder because the stressed dog is afraid to go to the toilet in front of you. What it doesn't do is teach your dog what he should be doing.

Punishment can also teach a dog that whatever was close to him when he was punished was the reason for the punishment, which means you

▼ If your dog raids the bin, move him away, then put the bin out of reach.

▲ If lots of children are running around, you could put your dog in a crate.

could end up with bigger problems than you started with. For example, if a child accidentally falls on and hurts a dog, which then growls – a perfectly natural response – followed by a telling-off from you, the dog will associate children with punishment. So, the next time a child goes near the dog, he will growl even louder. Again, you might shout and smack him, and eventually your dog is left with no choice but to bite the child to get them away.

The best way to avoid this problem is to move the dog out of the way when children are running around, and so avoid a potential accident. This brings us to the crucial subject of how a dog should be punished.

THE IMPORTANCE OF TIMING

For punishment to work effectively, your timing has to be perfect. You need to make sure that the dog associates the punishment with the crime that he has committed. If you do use punishment, you should use it only once, and it has to stop the behaviour once and for all. However, it would be better to teach your dog what you would like him to do instead.

▲ *If carried out correctly, 'time out' is a quick and effective measure.*

Because owners don't really want to punish their dogs, they sometimes use a small amount of punishment first. Then, when that doesn't work, the level of punishment is increased, and so on, until it ends up with a vicious smack. This is not a good idea, because you are causing unnecessary stress to you dog, and you are also hardening him to your punishing methods. However, you should not give up and ignore your dog's bad behaviour. The dog won't stop; he'll just become more practised at it.

Without using physical punishment, the question is: how do you teach your dog that he can't always do whatever he wants?

'TIME OUT'

Taking a quick break and walking away from your dog is a good way of stopping unwanted behaviour. Being a very mild form of punishment, it won't have any repercussions. If your timing is right, the dog will understand exactly what you don't want, and this method will sort out behavioural problems very quickly.

To use 'time out' effectively, you have to be quick and fair, either getting up quickly and walking away (not running) from your dog, or moving him to another room. Give your dog a cue to what's happening by saying firmly, "that's enough", without shouting. This isn't threatening or nagging, and it avoids the highly overused "no". So, when your dog begins to display unwanted behaviour, for example barking to get attention, say "that's enough" very calmly, take your dog out the nearest door and put him on a house line (a long thin lead that is attached to his collar at all times when you are in the house). Using a house line will mean that getting hold of your dog does not become a game of chase. Leave him out for 1 minute at the most, then let him back in. If he repeats the unwanted behaviour, repeat the action until he eventually realizes the connection between his behaviour and the consequences (separation from you).

BE CONSISTENT

If you are consistent and persistent, you'll remedy the problem within 2 weeks at the most. If your dog is exhibiting attention-seeking behaviour because you are too busy to spend time with him, you need to change your lifestyle. But attention-seeking behaviour does not just happen because you do not spend time with your dog. Sometimes it's quite the contrary. It doesn't matter how much time you spend with your dog, he may still learn to attention-seek.

The point to stress is that we can't control a dog's behaviour; we can only influence his behaviour by adjusting our actions. Make an effort to reward

Attention-seeking behaviour

If your dog's unwanted behaviour is attention-seeking, get up and walk out of the room immediately. Such behaviour includes:
• Mouthing, where your dog grabs at your wrists, hands or ankles
• Pawing
• Nudging you with his muzzle
• Begging
• Mounting inappropriate objects
• Stealing items and running away to initiate a game of chase
• Barking at you

the positive behaviour that you want. Don't fall into the trap of only noticing your dog when he behaves badly; that will simply make him repeat the bad behaviour to get your attention next time. Hence, chasing after a dog that is running around the garden with a towel is just a game to him, and won't make him stop.

▲ *With consistent training, your dog will settle when you want him to.*

Using rewards effectively

To get the best out of your dog when training him, you should reward good behaviour and the desired responses with either a small piece of food or by playing a game with him with his favourite toy, and with praise. As far as a dog is concerned, probably nothing beats the food reward, with praise at the bottom of the list.

TYPES OF REWARD

Garlic sausage may work wonders because it has a strong smell and taste that most dogs enjoy. But not every dog likes food treats. Some dogs are fussy eaters, and you have to be quite creative to find the right reward. Others are so food-obsessed that they'll find it hard to think about anything else if they can see what you're holding in your hand. So keep treats out of sight, then give them with lightning speed so that your dog can't see what else you've got.

▼ *Use small, easily chewable treats as an incentive to repeat good behaviour.*

It's also sensible to carry out dog training after your dog has eaten, so that he's not too hungry. If you feel that he is getting too many rewards, you could always use smaller treats.

PHASING OUT FOOD TREATS

Some people argue against using food rewards because they think their dog will need such rewards all the time, but this is not true. Once your dog understands how he's supposed to respond to a command, he'll instinctively do it and the reward system can be phased out. When it comes to commands such as 'fetch', the reward is your playing with him. That's all he needs. With you throwing a ball again and again, who needs food? That just slows things up!

▲ *Use tempting treats during training, such as pieces of cheese, cooked sausage and home-made liver cake.*

WHEN TO USE REWARDS

By using rewards effectively, you can teach your dog that the things he finds frightening are actually not a problem. So, a trip to the vet to have his claws cut can actually become a pleasurable experience, and instead of barking loudly every time the front doorbell rings, he'll be able to sit quietly while

Food rewards

Tasty edible rewards include:
- Small pieces of cheese
- Frankfurters
- Carrots
- Chicken
- Liver cake
- Tuna cake
- Sausage
- Anything your children leave on their dinner plates
- Pieces of fruit, if your dog enjoys it

▼ *Most dogs can be motivated by the reward of playing with their toys.*

▶ *Choose exciting rewards that you know your dog really wants.*

you see who's there. If he pulls toward something while he's on the lead, take a couple of steps back and get him back to your side before you walk again; if he keeps the lead loose, he can have what he wants. It's also worth making sure that he sits nicely while you're putting his lead on, when he's at the door waiting to go outside and while you prepare his dinner.

VARY THE REWARDS
Finding out what your dog loves and what he sees as rewarding is initially guesswork. It's best to use more boring rewards in the home, and the most exciting kinds outside when you're competing for your dog's attention with playful dogs, children playing ball and puddles to splash in. Also try to vary the rewards. If your

dog keeps getting the same reward – even tasty sausage – he will eventually get bored with it. The reward won't be a "Wow!" anymore, but "Is that the best you can do?"

When using food treats, choose those that are soft and easily cut into small pieces, so that your dog can eat them quickly. Hard biscuits take time and make training sessions last longer.

◀ *Vary the types of rewards you use. Most dogs enjoy playing tug-of-war.*

▶ *Verbal praise for a job well done, together with a pat and a stroke, is a good alternative to using food treats and toys.*

Clicker training

One of the most effective ways to train a dog is to use a clicker. This is a small box that makes a 'click-click' sound, and is always used to mean 'you've just done the right thing'. The clicker doesn't have an off-day or sound cross, and can be used when your dog is some distance from you. Once your dog understands a clicker, the rest is easy.

To introduce the clicker to your dog, put a treat under his nose, lure him into the sit position and, when his bottom hits the floor, click and give him the treat. Then move a couple of steps away from him so that he has to stand and follow you, and then lure him into a sit position, click when his bottom hits the floor, click again and reward him. Again, move away and, when your dog follows you, show him the treat in your hand and then close it and wait to see if he sits. If he does, click and give him a few treats. Once he is going into position when you show him the treat, you can say "Sit" as his bottom hits the floor.

There are many benefits to using the clicker, and the moment your dog can reliably follow your commands, you can put it aside.

▼ *Use a clicker to show approval of your dog's behaviour.*

INTRODUCING THE CLICKER

1 To introduce the clicker, hold a small food treat under your dog's nose when he is standing up. Hold the clicker in your other hand.

2 Lure your dog into the sit position by slowly moving the hand with the food treat above your dog's head. As your hand moves up, your dog should sit.

3 When the dog's bottom hits the floor, click the clicker. You should not point the clicker directly at your dog, nor hold it too close to his ear.

4 As soon as you click the clicker, reward your dog with the food treat. He will begin to associate the clicker sound with doing the right thing.

5 Repeat the process two or three times more, moving a couple of steps away so that your dog follows you.

6 Show your dog the food treat, then close your hand and wait for him to offer a sit.

7 Be patient and wait him out; it may take a while. When his bottom hits the floor, immediately click the clicker.

8 The first time he gets it right on his own, reward him heavily with a food treat and plenty of praise.

HOW TO BEGIN

You've scoured the Internet, reading everything on your chosen breed, and you know all about the behavioural characteristics and ultimate size of your dog. You know that your new puppy will fit perfectly into your lifestyle. You've also looked into the best training classes and bought all the equipment you need. Now it's time to learn the basics of dog training. It's up to you to find what motivates your dog, and to make sure he's given an appropriate reward that will ensure he does what he's told. With the right training, any problems can be put right. So, if your puppy does not come back when called, it's simply because the pleasure of playing with other dogs or foraging in the undergrowth outscores the reward he knows he'll get from you. If you always give him a big treat, however, he'll return quickly enough. It's up to you to be consistent in your training.

◄ *Training your dog when you are out and about will help to build a good relationship, and will give you the chance to praise and reward him.*

Bringing your puppy home

You've bought the lead, bowl, bed, toys, crate and how-to books. You've told the children not to pester your puppy, and you've taken a week off work to settle him in. You're ready. What next?

PUPPY-PROOFING

The first thing you need to do is look around each room in your house and think about safety. Making your home puppy-proof takes time and thought, and you need to conceal a number of dangerous objects. Start with wires and cables behind computers, televisions and telephones, because if chewed, they can be hazardous and could even kill your puppy. Then move everything that is at a low level in the house, including plants, shoes and children's toys. Look around the house and imagine you're a playful puppy. What can you destroy?

COLLECTING YOUR PUPPY

The best time to collect your puppy from the breeders is mid-morning. This will give him time to digest his breakfast, so that he's not sick in the car. Put him in a small dog basket or cardboard box lined with a blanket, and secure it. When he arrives home, he may be scared and refuse to eat, and if you have children, they may be overexcited. Your puppy may defecate on the carpet, but don't panic. He is under a great deal of stress, having just left his mother and siblings.

SETTLING IN

As soon as you get your puppy home, take him outside and let him get a feel for his surroundings, but stay with him at all times. If he goes to the toilet, praise him. If he doesn't, take him outside every 10 minutes until you get a result, then praise him.

▲ *It's exciting bringing a puppy home, but it can be stressful for the puppy.*

Help him settle in by keeping the house quiet and the children under control. Put his crate or bed in a quiet corner where he can be left in peace to sleep. Also, let him settle for a few days before letting friends see him. Don't be alarmed if he gets a runny tummy – this is likely to be part of the stress of settling in. Make sure he keeps to the diet provided by the breeder, otherwise you could inadvertently make things worse.

Have a selection of strong toys for your puppy to play with. But give him plenty of time to rest, because a young puppy needs lots of sleep. Make sure

◀ *Allow your puppy time to explore and get used to his new surroundings.*

▼ *Provide the new puppy with his own bed in a quiet corner of the kitchen.*

that children leave him alone when he's resting – a tired puppy will be a grumpy puppy.

Don't be in a rush to take your puppy to the vet for his first vaccination. Let him build a bond with you first, so that his first trip to the vet is minimally stressful.

PUPPY'S FIRST NIGHT

The first night could be a trying time if it isn't properly planned. Not only is his environment new, but it is almost certainly the first time he has slept without his litter mates. Let your puppy go to the toilet, then put him in his crate, turn the light off and close the door. But what if he starts whining? Don't ignore him – he will be lonely and missing the familiar sounds, smell and warmth of his litter mates. For the first few nights, until he settles in, you could let him sleep in his crate next to your bed. If you don't like that arrangement, sleep on the sofa with him beside you in his crate for a couple of nights.

Sleeping close to him also means that you'll hear him if he wakes in the

night needing the toilet, and you can take him out. This will greatly help with house-training. Puppies have very small bladders and need to go to the toilet much more often than you might think. It should take less than a week for him to sleep on his own in his crate in the kitchen.

If he still cries in the night, do not shout at him – this would cause stress and anxiety. Instead, put your fingers though the crate to soothe him back to sleep, or wrap a hot water bottle in a towel and put that in his bed. You

▲ *A playful puppy needs a good supply of suitable chew toys.*

could also try turning on the radio. Soft music is very comforting. Silence can be frightening for a puppy if he is used to the snuffling and snores of the rest of the litter.

When he wakes up the next morning, take him straight outside again so that he can relieve himself. Carry him out, because walking that distance may encourage him to go inside the house.

◄ *On his first night, put your puppy in his crate. If he cries in the night, soothe him back to sleep.*

▶ *Carry your puppy into the garden the next morning, so that he can begin house-training.*

House-training

This is the most crucial task with a new puppy. Hopefully the breeder will have begun taking the puppies into the garden to get them used to going to the toilet outside. What you shouldn't do is encourage your puppy to go inside, even on newspaper. You must also be alert to his signals, understanding when he needs to go, because when a puppy is desperate, he can't wait.

◄ *Reward your puppy for being quiet in his crate – feed him small food treats for good behaviour. It is helpful if he learns to sleep in a crate as he is unlikely to foul his sleeping place.*

HOW OFTEN?

The frequency with which your puppy will need to go to the toilet depends on several factors, first his diet. If you use dried food, he'll drink more water than when eating wet food, prompting more visits outside. Second, if you buy cheaper dog food with cheaper ingredients, it usually makes a great deal more waste and so, again, your puppy will need to go to the toilet more often. Third, the size of your puppy influences the number of visits to the toilet, with a small breed needing to go more often than a large dog, because the former has a smaller bladder.

HOUSE-TRAINING USING A FENCED-OFF AREA

1 Take your puppy on his lead to an area designated as his toilet – ideally a fenced-off area of the garden.

2 Reward him with a small food treat as soon as he goes. It's important to do this the moment he has finished.

HOUSE-TRAINING METHODS

Training your puppy not to go to the toilet in the house takes time, and there are bound to be some accidents along the way. It helps to get your puppy to sleep in a crate, because he won't want to foul his sleeping place. Introduce your puppy to the crate by feeding him in it, giving him treats there and lying him down in it when he's sleepy. Make sure that the moment he starts whining, you take him outside.

If your puppy does have an accident inside, do not punish him, because that will make him wary of going to the toilet in front of you, and house-training will then become very difficult. He'll probably end up going where you can't see him – even in a handbag.

To begin with, take your puppy out soon after he has woken up, after he has eaten, after playtime, when he's excited and every 45 minutes. Make sure he knows which is his toilet area in the garden, especially if you have young children; you don't want your children wading through piles of

▲ *Buy a special cleaner from a pet shop for cleaning up after your puppy.*

faeces on the lawn. Fence off a small toilet area and take your puppy there on the lead, rewarding him enthusiastically when he does what's expected. Give him a small treat, but it's crucial that you get the timing right: reward him the moment he has finished going to the toilet.

Some puppies give signs that they are about to go, and they may begin sniffing the carpet or floor, circling or squatting. When this happens, clap your hands to get your puppy's attention, and encourage him to follow you out the door. If he really is about to go, pick him up and take him outside very quickly.

CLEANING UP

If your puppy does have an accident, treat the site with a cleaner specifically designed for the job. This will remove the scent of urine. If the odour is left, your puppy will think that's his toilet, and will be attracted there by the smell in future. Note that household cleaners and disinfectants don't usually remove the scent, they just mask it, so you do need to use a special cleaner available from good pet shops.

OTHER OPTIONS

If you need to leave your puppy alone for long periods, you won't have any option but to use puppy pads, which are specifically designed to soak up urine, or sheets of newspaper on the floor, but at least make sure he understands what the pads or paper are for. As with house-training, every time he shows any inclination to go to the toilet, put him on the pads or newspaper. Dog flaps are not suitable because young puppies don't understand the concept of going out to the toilet and should not be unattended outside.

TRAINING A PUPPY TO RING A BELL

You could also teach him to try to go on command, which is very useful if you are taking him out for the day or visiting friends, but you must use the command just as he's going to the toilet, so that he makes the correct association between the two events.

RINGING A BELL

If your puppy isn't very good at asking to go out, you can teach him to ring a bell. It's an easy little trick. All you need is a small, light bell. Hang it on a piece of string so that it is dangling at about nose height for your puppy. When you walk him to the door to let him out, ring the bell immediately before you open the door. He'll associate the door opening with the ringing bell. In future, he should ring it if he wants to go. When you go on holiday, take the bell with you.

1 Attach a bell to a piece of string and hang it from the back door, making sure it is at nose height for your puppy.

2 Ring the bell before you open the door to let him out. In time, he should ring it himself when he wants to go.

Handling and grooming

From an owner's, a vet's and a groomer's point of view, being able to handle your pet is vital. It makes it easy for everyone to do their job, so that the dog doesn't have to be pinned down (which is alarming for both pet and owner), and ensures that the dog is relaxed. If the dog feels nervous and threatened, on the other hand, he might bite.

BENEFITS OF HANDLING AND GROOMING

About 20 per cent of dog bites are directed at the owner's hand when they are trying to grasp their dog's collar, while many children have their faces bitten when they try to give their dog a hug. Research has shown that dogs that have been handled by many different people when they are puppies become better socialized and are rarely aggressive with people or

▼ *If your dog is used to being handled, vet visits will not be so traumatic.*

other dogs. If you train your dog to tolerate being handled, the number of bites will be a lot lower.

Getting him used to being handled regularly also means you can feel if there are any lumps and bumps emerging, locating potential health problems at an early age. For an illness to be diagnosed correctly, a dog needs to be happy with an invasive examination.

One advantage of checking your dog's teeth, for example, is that if he picks something up in his mouth that is dangerous, you'll be able to get it back without a fight. Sometimes twigs get trapped between the teeth, and you should be able to get these out without too much fuss. Likewise, if you need to give your dog medication or handle him when he's in pain, he shouldn't see that as a threat.

Similarly, getting your dog used to grooming means that you'll be able to wipe the mud from his feet and comb

▲ *Grooming your dog several times a week gets him used to being handled.*

out tangled knots without any fuss. It is equally as important to groom a short-haired dog as a long-haired one, to get rid of any dead hair.

Regular grooming will help eliminate fleas or ticks that might cause health problems, but it should not be limited to giving your dog a quick going-over with a brush. Get him accustomed to having his teeth, ears, eyes, paws and area under the tail examined so that when he has to go to the vet to get his temperature taken, it will not be such a shock.

BE GENTLE

Not all dogs are instinctively happy at being examined closely. Some like having their ears and tummy stroked, but draw the line at having their feet or teeth examined. Don't make this a battle, forcing the dog's mouth open, because you'll alarm and possibly even hurt him. It also means that next

▲ *It is important to be able to regularly clip your dog's claws without stress.*

time you go near him, he'll know what's coming and try to warn you off with a snarl and maybe even a bite. Be gentle, rewarding your dog at each stage. Let him realize that nothing awful is happening. Build up his confidence. It doesn't matter if it takes several sessions before he lets you check his teeth. There's no rush.

HOW TO BEGIN

The best way to get your dog used to being handled closely is to begin by stroking him gently, letting him get used to the feel of you. With a young puppy that tries to bite, wait until he is tired. While you are stroking him, play around with his ears and have a look inside them. Stroke him down the front legs and gently feel between his toes. If he pulls his foot away, he needs to be desensitized to your touch. If he

▶ *Build up your dog's confidence by praising him while gently handling his paws.*

doesn't like you looking at his teeth – and not many dogs do to begin with – again you need to desensitize him to your handling. Let him lick a piece of cheese held between your thumb and finger, and lift his lip up to look at his teeth while he is busy.

You could also try smearing some soft cheese on the refrigerator door or, if you have a tiled floor, squash some cheese on to the surface so that while your puppy is busy licking it off, you can examine him thoroughly, including his back, belly and under his tail. When he is happy to let you handle him, get your friends to give him a once-over. If you have children, you can supervise them, but make sure they are gentle. If your puppy complains or pulls away from any area being handled, reward him well when he lets you touch him there. Be especially gentle around his mouth while he is a puppy, because his gums may hurt when he is losing his puppy teeth and the adult teeth are coming through.

▲ *Get your dog used to handling his mouth so you can look at his teeth.*

▲ *Reward him with a tasty treat when he lets you check him all over.*

▼ *Once he is used to being handled, he should enjoy being towel-dried after he gets muddy during his walk.*

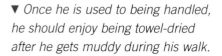

Socialization and habituation

Puppies need to be socialized so that they are happy meeting other puppies and adult dogs, people of both sexes, children, babies in pushchairs, older people and people in wheelchairs. The list is endless. It is important to note that the socialization window is only open for a short time – up to the age of 14 weeks – so you need to make the most of it to ensure your puppy doesn't have problems when he's an adult. Make all such encounters enjoyable, asking adults who are new to him to toss him a few treats.

SOCIALIZATION

Your breeder should already have begun the socialization process, with the puppy being handled regularly on a daily basis. If you have a busy household, your puppy will already have become used to household appliances, visitors and the hustle and bustle of day-to-day noise. If you have a quieter home, you will have to put more time and effort into exposing him to different experiences.

BEFORE 12 WEEKS

There are several things your puppy should be introduced to before he's 12 weeks old. First, when he has settled down, invite visitors of all ages to meet him. Keep him quiet when they arrive so that he learns to be calm when people are around. If you don't have children, ask friends who do have them to visit, but make sure they are well briefed and don't get your puppy overexcited.

Put something tasty in your puppy's food dish so that he gets used to people being around when he eats.

Groom and handle your puppy every day. Look in his ears, at his teeth and between his pads. Also get other people to handle your puppy, so that when he has to visit the vet, he isn't frightened. He needs to get used to wearing his collar too.

▲ *Children should be taught how to care for their dog's needs by grooming and handling them. Start the process before your puppy is 12 weeks old.*

HABITUATION

This is the name given to a natural process of learning by repetitive exposure to a stimulus. For example, a puppy may be frightened of the noise of a washing machine, but each time the machine is turned on, his reaction will diminish. Eventually, he will show no reaction to the noise at all, and he has become 'habituated' to it. Habituation to a wide range of items and experiences is vital for the young puppy, and the process will continue throughout his lifetime.

◄ *Cats and dogs can live in harmony, especially if they grow up together.*

▲ *Stay with your puppy when he is eating; he will get used to people around his food bowl.*

▲ *Giving your puppy a weekly health check will prepare him for his first visits to the vet's or the groomer's.*

▲ *Carrying your puppy everywhere you go will habituate him to the environment in which you live.*

Habituation can also be used as a training tool. If your puppy becomes overexcited when you pick up his lead, it is because he expects to go for a walk. But if you take the lead with you every time you leave the house, he will soon come to realize that the act of picking up the lead is not a signal for walk time.

TOWN AND COUNTRY

Carry your puppy out to meet the postman, so that he won't bark at him. If you live in a town, try to take your puppy into the countryside, but keep him under strict control so that he learns to leave wildlife and livestock alone. Reward him for obeying your commands and staying with you. Never let him off the lead when around livestock. Remember that a farmer has the right to shoot your dog for worrying his animals, especially

▶ *If your puppy gets used to horses early, he will behave well around them.*

sheep around lambing time. If you live in the countryside, it is imperative that you carry your puppy around the nearest town to get him used to all the sights and sounds. Initially go when it is quiet, gradually building up to busier periods. Before his vaccinations, before he is around

12 weeks of age, it is important that you don't let your puppy walk outside in parks and fields that are visited by other dogs – he might get a fatal disease. However, you can carry him with you everywhere you go, and he can visit friends' houses whose dogs have been vaccinated.

Puppy classes and puppy parties

There are two main ways in which your local veterinary surgery can help when your puppy is ready to meet other animals and get used to going to the vet: puppy classes and puppy parties. The former provide professional advice and training for new puppies, with information about vaccinations and health, basic training and how to deal with common problems such as house-training and biting.

A puppy party, on the other hand, is an informal gathering of puppies and their owners at the local vet's. The intention is a good one: to enable puppies to socialize with each other at the same time as getting used to the vet's surgery. The idea is that puppies are put on the examination table, given a treat and are played with by the staff, all of which helps to ensure that future vet visits are relaxed. That is the theory, but unfortunately the reality can actually be a nightmare. Aspects of classes and parties can be combined.

▼ *Staff at the vet's will be more than happy to give puppies a cuddle.*

PUPPY CLASSES

When looking for a good puppy class, ask your friends for recommendations, and ask the trainer if you can go along to watch first. Look for one that is run exclusively for puppies, with no more than eight puppies to a class, with one trainer and an assistant.

▼ *If you reassure your puppy, the vet's should not become a place to fear.*

▲ *Introduce your puppy to the vet so he gets used to visiting the surgery.*

The class should be a mixture of advice and training, with the vet or the nurse giving a short talk on worming, vaccinations, diet, general care and other health-related matters. You should also have a chance to ask any niggling questions about puppy care and be able to talk to other owners.

The puppies should be let off the lead two at a time, the pairs being determined by temperament and size. Shy puppies should be twinned together, being praised when they are brave enough to greet and initiate play with their new friend. They must be given time, without fear of being ambushed by another puppy twice as big. Puppies that are not involved should sit on their owner's knees while they wait their turn.

This is also an excellent time for you to learn about the small nuances of a dog's body language and dog-to-dog communication. The class should cover all the basics, showing you how

▶ *If you have litter mates, encourage them to play with you and not just with each other.*

to teach your dog to sit, lie, come when called and walk on a loose lead. The trainer should also be able to help you solve problems concerning house-training, biting, tantrums and diet.

OBEDIENCE TRAINING

Some puppy classes go one step further and concentrate on competition obedience, where they insist that your dog walks on a certain side, doing about-turns etc. If you want to take part in obedience competitions, that's fine, but in the real world it's not always easy to keep your dog on your inner side (if you are walking along the road it's natural to keep your dog on the side that's furthest away from the traffic). Good classes will offer flexibility to suit you.

▼ *Give your puppy small food treats as a reward for good behaviour and to encourage it to continue.*

PUPPY PARTIES

Unfortunately, just like dog training, you don't need a qualification to hold a puppy party and, if the puppies aren't properly supervised, the event can easily become an off-putting experience. First, the average surgery waiting room is far too small for lots of puppies all off the lead together. Second, if there isn't adequate supervision, bullying can occur. Leaving the puppies to 'sort it out for themselves' is unfair, with the

▼ *It's important that your puppy learns to be relaxed with strangers. Ask other owners to handle him.*

bullied desperate to find a hiding place and the bullies getting a taste for it, while the shy animals simply have their shyness reinforced.

In these situations, puppies don't learn to become more confident – those that have had a bad experience won't relish meeting other dogs next time you're in the park. But it doesn't have to be like this. With good supervision, puppy parties can actually be positive for young dogs.

Some puppy parties are sponsored by well-known companies. Veterinary surgeries use the parties as an advertisement for their services. Therefore, it is in the best interests of both to ensure the parties are well run. In addition, a good number of vets offer staff courses as part of their team's professional development.

A good puppy party offers early socializing in a safe environment. Not only do the puppies see new sights and sounds, but advice is available on a range of veterinary and nutritional issues. It is an opportunity for puppies to interact with each other and for owners to discuss any issues that concern them. Puppy parties can offer a confidence-gaining experience to both owner and pet. Go and watch a puppy party first to make sure it is well run. Do this without your puppy.

Play is important

As well as being a great relationship builder, playing with your puppy is also the perfect way to incorporate some training into his fun time. For example, tug-of-war, when played properly, is a great way of teaching your dog self-control, how to give things up easily and the consequences of accidentally getting hold of clothing or skin (which should immediately end the game). It's also a great way to build up teamwork, and if the weather is poor, you can get him to expend some energy indoors. Even more importantly, it's a good way to practise your 'leave it' and 'drop it' commands, as well as 'sit' (if he gets overexcited) and 'wait'. To some breeds of dog, a game of tug will override any other reward. Terriers love it, which is why it should definitely become part of their training sessions.

TUG-OF-WAR

If your dog doesn't know how to play tug-of-war, it's very easy to teach him. Using a ragger, tempt your dog to chase it by wiggling it along the floor. When he chases and gets hold of it, praise him, then toss it away and let him fetch it. Take hold of the other end and give it a gentle tug, then let go. If your dog runs away with the ragger, don't chase him. Let him have it. He'll bring it back to you soon enough when he wants you to play some more.

Once your dog knows how to play tug, you can implement some rules and make it part of your training. If he gets overexcited when you get the tug toy out, hide it behind your back until he sits patiently, thus teaching him a bit of self-control. If he responds well

▲ *Older children and dogs can enjoy playing tug-of-war together.*

when you get it out, hide it behind your back and ask your dog to sit. When he sits, the ragger becomes the reward. Then give the command "take it" when he grabs it, have a good tug and then hold a treat right under his nose. When he lets go of the ragger to get the treat, say "drop it". After a few games, you should be able to make him drop the toy by holding a treat under his nose. If he accidentally grabs

◄ *Dogs enjoy playing with other dogs, but they need to be supervised at all times.*

▶ *Many dogs enjoy chasing and retrieving objects, and the game becomes an excellent bonding exercise.*

hold of clothing or skin by mistake, drop the ragger and walk away so that he realizes he has made an error.

CHOOSE SUITABLE GAMES

It is important that you don't win the game all the time; it's not much fun for the dog to keep losing. It used to be said that if a dog wins he will become dominant, but actually nothing could be further from the truth. The whole object of playing tug is that it is fun for both parties.

This explains why, in general, you shouldn't let young children play tug with your puppy – there's too much potential for accidents and overexcitement. The same applies to chasing games, and if you have any of the herding breeds (for example, a collie or shepherd), they may nip the children's ankles.

Wrestling games are also unsuitable, with puppies either becoming too rough, or if you try wrestling with a shy puppy, it might actually make him become even more timid.

TRAINING A PUPPY TO PLAY TUG-OF-WAR

1 Begin by wiggling a colourful ragger along the floor to get your puppy's attention, tempting him to start playing.

2 Your puppy should chase the ragger, jump on it and then start chewing it. Praise him for doing this.

3 Toss the ragger a short distance away from you for your puppy to chase. Encourage him to bring it back to you.

4 Let him play with the ragger without chasing him. When he brings it back, play with him and repeat the process.

5 Let your puppy win the tug-of-war game sometimes, allowing him time to chew the ragger on his own.

Building confidence in the shy dog

Puppies can be shy for all kinds of reasons, ranging from being genetically predisposed to shyness, being the runt of the litter, or a bad upbringing by an unsympathetic family and/or a spell in a rescue centre. But, whatever the reason, shyness needs to be dealt with promptly before it leads to problems of fear and aggression, such as lunging at whoever or whatever alarms the dog.

HOW YOU CAN HELP

If you have an older dog with a confidence problem, rehabilitation will take more time and patience, because you need to change his association of what is scary to what's acceptable or even fun. It is best to hire a dog trainer who can help you, and who will teach you his body language signals so that you'll know whether he is coping.

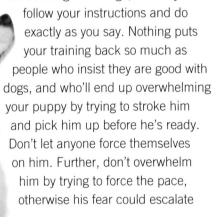

▶ *Don't rush your shy puppy – let him investigate his surroundings and get to know family members at his own pace.*

The shy puppy can be helped by you, but each day you must go at his pace, never rushing him, gently coaxing him along and being ready to break off when it's clear he's had enough. Having friends who can help will be a big advantage, but they must follow your instructions and do exactly as you say. Nothing puts your training back so much as people who insist they are good with dogs, and who'll end up overwhelming your puppy by trying to stroke him and pick him up before he's ready. Don't let anyone force themselves on him. Further, don't overwhelm him by trying to force the pace, otherwise his fear could escalate

◀ *Some dogs are naturally shy, and may hide under the furniture until they feel more sure of their surroundings.*

▼ *Lack of early socialization will lead to shyness, but with time you can build confidence.*

into a phobia. Tell your friends to sit down before you bring him in, and let your puppy investigate them rather than the other way around.

Let the puppy make all the moves. Praise him for any confident behaviour, but ignore him when he shows signs of fearfulness. If you punish him for his fearful behaviour, this will only escalate the problem. While it's human nature to comfort those who are upset, if you do that to the dog, he'll think you are rewarding

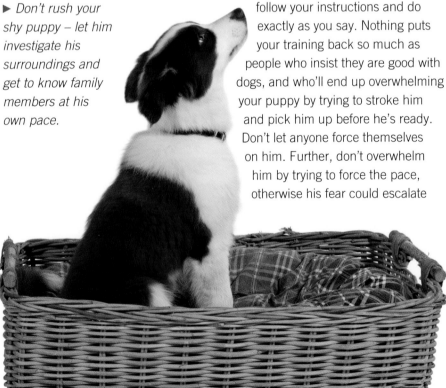

◄ *Reward and praise any brave behaviour shown by a shy dog.*

▼ *Introduce your puppy to as many people as possible while he is young.*

his shyness. Working with a shy puppy takes time and patience, but the reward of seeing his increased confidence is worth the effort invested.

BUILDING CONFIDENCE OUTDOORS
Beware of strangers coming up to you when you are out with your shy puppy, wanting to say hello and give him a cuddle. He may well find this overwhelming and end up giving them a nasty bite. Instead, you could ask a friendly stranger to give your puppy a treat. Even if the puppy seems

reluctant, don't give up; keep trying. Eventually he'll become increasingly at ease with new people.

While the shy dog may never become an extrovert, there are many things you can do to help him become more confident. Concentrate on rewarding any aspect of good behaviour, and it will boost your puppy's confidence.

SET REALISTIC GOALS
You need to be realistic when socializing your shy puppy. Nothing is more detrimental then swamping him

with too many potentially frightening experiences at once. Take small steps toward you goal, and build confidence gradually.

Progression should be made by first choosing a quiet place such as a bench in the park, and just sitting and watching. When your puppy is totally relaxed in this situation, try walking around the park. Next, walk down a quiet road, then choose a busier one, until finally over a period of days, weeks or months he is able to cope with a bustling environment.

◄ *Socialization is vitally important with a shy dog. Praise him when strangers are walking nearby.*

▶ *Using rewards will teach your puppy that there is no need to be scared of strange people.*

Teaching your puppy his name

When you are out with your dog, you need to be able to communicate with him when he is off the lead playing with other dogs or sniffing in the undergrowth. Calling out his name means you can get his attention, possibly giving him his next command like "come here, time to go home" or "leave it" if he is eating something unsavoury, chasing a jogger or pestering children playing football.

▼ *Teaching a puppy his name means you can always get his attention.*

WHY A NAME IS IMPORTANT

When you say your dog's name, you want him to look at you expectantly and wait for the next command. The importance of getting a puppy to respond to his name cannot be stressed enough. If something scares him and he flees, he might dash toward a main road; getting him to return promptly could save his life.

It's no surprise that most puppies think their name is 'No' by the time they are 4 months old; it's one of the most over-used words with puppies and dogs. It's far better to teach your puppy to respond to his name and then give a command, rather than just shouting "no".

At the other extreme, children often excitedly say their puppy's name over and over again when trying to get his attention, but this becomes so over-used that it means nothing to the puppy and just becomes background noise. So, when you do call your puppy by name, make it a rewarding experience. Don't call him to tell him off because he is having a good chew on your shoes or to make him do something he'll hate, like having a bath, or he will associate the sound of his name with trouble and run away.

TEACHING A NAME

Several times a day, take the time to teach your puppy his name, using a handful of treats or a toy that he loves. Put him on the lead so that he can't wander off. Toss a small treat on the floor just a short distance away from you and let him eat it. Just as he has finished, say his name. If he looks up at you, praise him and tell him he is a good boy.

▲ *Your puppy needs to be able to answer to his name when in the park.*

If he ignores you, don't say his name. The object of the exercise is to get your puppy to look at you the first time you say his name.

If he does not respond to the sound of his name the first time you say it, that's probably because he doesn't understand what his name means. You need to get his attention another way, either by clapping your hands, slapping the floor or tapping him on the bottom. As soon as he turns to look at you, tell him he's a good boy and reward him. Four or five times, toss a treat or toy away from you, get your dog to look somewhere else and then see if he will look at you when you say his name. Go through this three or four times a day, and eventually he should immediately respond to his name every time.

The same method is used if you're re-naming an older dog. Some people think you can't change a dog's name, but this is untrue. A name is only a sound to a dog; he doesn't understand the actual word. Rescue dogs may have had several names before gaining a permanent home. You can ensure they respond to their new name by following the three training steps on this page.

Once your puppy really understands the sound of his name, don't ruin it by trying words like 'biscuit', especially if he's slow to respond. Why? Because this teaches him that his name means nothing, whereas the word 'biscuit' is significant. You need to reinforce the fact that his name really does mean something.

ADDING DISTRACTIONS

The next stage is to add distractions to your training so that when your puppy is busy doing something else, he will still respond to your call. Distract him by inviting people to your house, letting him play with children, allowing him to run around the garden and giving him new toys. When he is

able to respond to his name in every situation, it's time to use his name when he is a short distance away in the park, when he is sniffing a tree or when he has just said hello to someone.

You need to teach your puppy that whatever he is doing when you say his name, he must respond. Always follow

▲ *Reward your puppy with a game when he responds to his name.*

up with a command. Just watch in the park and see how many owners use the dog's name and expect him to understand that it actually means 'come here'. You need to be very clear to your dog what you want him to do.

TEACHING YOUR PUPPY HIS NAME

1 Toss a small food treat on to the floor a short distance away from you, keeping your puppy on a lead.

2 Allow your puppy to reach the treat and let him eat it. Just as he finishes eating the treat, say his name.

3 If he looks at you, praise him. If he ignores you, do not reward him; repeat the process until he does look at you.

Adolescent dogs

It is no surprise that the majority of dogs in rescue centres are adolescents, between the ages of 6 months and 2 years. Like humans, dogs are at their most challenging during adolescence, when they're bombarded by hormones.

THE URGE TO CHEW

Your cute puppy will suddenly become gangly as he goes through a rapid growth stage, possibly accompanied by growing pains. To make matters worse, he'll have a strong urge to chew things as his adult teeth bed down in the gums. So, just when you thought you'd got through the puppy chewing stage, it starts all over again, only this time the teeth are bigger and capable of doing more serious damage. For this reason, you can't have too many chew toys. Buy new ones if those he had as a puppy are now outgrown.

▼ *Adolescent dogs need to chew, and they also love playing with other dogs.*

HORMONAL CHANGES

Sex also comes high on the agenda as bitches head toward their first season, and a male's testosterone begins to reach new heights. The adolescent male has more testosterone than an adult dog, and your obedient puppy will be replaced by a sex-mad, hormonal teenager. He may chase after bitches and fight males, or become fearful of dogs that he once played with nicely. Worse, he may ignore your commands. It's not surprising that some owners give up and hand their adolescent dogs into rescue centres, because the problems can seem insurmountable.

It's very tempting to put your dog back on the lead at this stage, but it's important to still let him play with other dogs. You'll quickly notice that your growing, confident dog charges toward other dogs with tail high, shoulders back and a swagger, whereas before he may have approached with his tail down and his head low. However, while older dogs will tolerate a great deal of raucous

▲ *During adolescence, puppies start to become more confident.*

puppy behaviour, they are less likely to tolerate rude adolescent behaviour, and you may find that your dog is being reprimanded by other dogs.

SOCIAL SKILLS

One way of maintaining your adolescent dog's social skills is by taking him to new places where he can meet new dogs. Most owners get into a fixed routine with their dogs too easily, taking the same route through the same parks, and meeting the same people with the same dogs. But an adolescent dog's social skills will quickly deteriorate if they don't get any variety.

It's worth adding that we sometimes expect too much of our dogs, and think they'll become instant best friends with every dog they meet. Certainly during adolescence there will be dog fights, sometimes over a bitch, but they are usually not serious – more a case of 'teeth and noise'. Fights tend to look worse than they are.

MALE ADOLESCENTS

Your adolescent male dog may begin to leave scent marks in great quantities over upright objects, including every lamp post and tree.

▼ *Male adolescent dogs urinate frequently to mark their scent.*

He may even disgrace himself and leave scent mark indoors or in a friend's house. Don't panic if he does; just re-train him by giving rewards when he goes to the toilet where you want him to. He may also become sexually aware and find mounting people's legs irresistible and very exciting. You might consider having him castrated, which can help.

FEMALE ADOLESCENTS

Bitches can be equally troublesome. When in season, they may become withdrawn and moody, get snappy with males that want to sniff their rear, and go off their food. If you own more than one bitch, keep an eye on them, because fights may develop.

A bitch's season can start at any time after 6 months, and the smaller the breed, the earlier the season begins. A bitch usually loses blood for 10 days, and it is then that she will

▼ *Developing males may try to mate by mounting a person's leg.*

▼ *Male adolescent dogs urinate frequently to mark their scent.*

want to mate with any available passing male. It is unfair to continue walking bitches in parks during this time, because they'll cause fights between male dogs.

Not only will your bitch be a bit tetchy when on heat, but she may well have a phantom pregnancy. She'll act like she's having puppies, may become grumpy, go off her food and carry around a particular toy as if it were a puppy. This can be very

distressing both for the bitch and the owner. Having your female puppy spayed after her first season will remedy this problem. If your bitch is really out of sorts, the vet can administer something to help, and if you plan to breed her but want to wait until she is more mature, see how her first season progresses, then decide.

▼ *Adolescents often sniff each other in the park. Watch out for fights.*

TRAINING BASIC COMMANDS

The simplest command to get your dog to obey is 'sit'. Get him to obey immediately and you'll avoid having an overexcited, yapping, leaping hooligan every time you have a visitor. If he can sit on cue and be calm, you can take him anywhere and he won't pester you for attention. When training your dog, it's best to start indoors in one room, then move to another room, then to the garden, and finish off by the roadside. But note that when you teach a dog to sit in one particular place, you may have to repeat the entire lesson to get him to sit in another room or outside. The length of each training session often depends on which breed of dog you have, with sight hounds and terriers benefiting from frequent, short sessions, while border collies and labradors perform better with relatively long (and fewer) sessions.

◄ *With patience, you can train your dog to enjoy responding to your cues. It is best to train little and often, gradually building up your dog's skills over time.*

Sit

▶ *Teaching your puppy to sit when he is off the lead is important.*

Teaching a dog to sit is relatively easy. You need to get your dog to do it on command, at a time when he might be interested in doing something much more interesting, such as snuffling through the undergrowth following some weird, enticing scent.

Have a handful of small treats. Hold one in front of your dog's nose, and move it upward and slightly backward toward his tail slowly, so that your dog's head moves up to follow the treat. You'll quickly see that as his head moves up, his bottom will go down. As soon as his bottom hits the floor, reward him and say "good boy". If your dog begins jumping up at your hand, you are holding the treat too far away from the front of his nose; put your hand behind your back until he settles down. When you start again, make sure the treat is right at the end of his nose.

Repeat this three or four times with a small treat, then let him have a rest. This stage needs to be repeated three or four times a day, and can easily be fitted in between television programmes and meals. The second time you try teaching a sit, if your dog's bottom hits the floor consistently, keep the treat in your hand behind your back and use your other hand to give the signals, moving it upward and backward toward his tail. Say "good boy" as his bottom hits the floor and reward him with the treat from your other hand.

The next stage is to make sure you say the word 'sit' as he is going into the sitting position – not a second before. Follow this up by checking that he understands what you are asking him. Hide the treat behind your back and tell him to sit. Does he do it the first time? If he stands looking at you, he doesn't understand, in which case you should go back to saying "sit" as he's going into the sitting position. Only proceed to the next stage when he sits immediately every time, on command.

You'll soon note that once you've said "good boy" or given him a treat, he stands up again. To get him to stay in the sitting position, initially withhold the treat for a couple of seconds, gradually making this period longer by several seconds before he gets his reward. Don't be too hard on him; make this an achievable feat.

The final stage of the lesson is getting your dog to sit by the roadside while you are talking to someone. If he ever hesitates, however, it is important to resist the urge to push down on his back. There are a couple of reasons for this: first, you may damage his developing bone structure; and second, he will usually offer some resistance, pushing back, which causes you to push harder and harder every time you want him to obey.

TRAINING A DOG TO SIT

1 Have a few small food treats ready. Hold one in front of your dog's nose and move it upwards and backwards.

2 As you move the treat toward your dog's tail, his head will move up and his bottom will move down. Say "sit".

3 As soon as your dog sits, reward him with the food treat. Repeat, gradually increasing the time before the reward.

Down

▶ *Once your dog has learned to sit, it is easy to train him to lie down.*

Teaching your dog to lie down on cue is another essential command, especially when you're in a friend's garden or sitting in an outdoor café. Like sitting, teaching him to lie down isn't usually difficult because it's such a natural movement, although some breeds (such as border collies) find it easier to do on command than others (such as sight hounds and whippets).

First, get your dog to sit in front of you, then hold a treat under his nose and move it in a straight line from under his nose to his paws on the floor. As soon as his chest hits the floor, reward and praise him. Only practise this about four or five times in each session, to keep him interested.

If you have a terrier, who finds it easier to go straight down from the

TRAINING A DOG TO LIE DOWN

1 Ask your dog to sit in front of you. When he is in the sit position, hold a small food treat under his nose.

2 Slowly lower the treat down in a straight line from his nose to his paws. While doing this, say "down".

3 As soon as your dog's chest hits the floor, give him the treat and praise him. Repeat the lesson four or five times.

standing position, again have the treat right under his nose and lure him down and slightly backward. If he goes down with his nose and front legs but leaves his rear in the air, resist the urge to push down on his bottom. Just hold the treat on the floor between your finger and thumb and wait, and he will eventually lie down or get up and walk away. If he does walk away, repeat the exercise but reward him for each stage that he completes successfully. So, if you reward him for putting his front end down first, he may well put his front end down and his chest, and before long he will be lying down. Be patient.

If you have a small dog or puppy that's having real trouble lying down, sit on the floor with your legs outstretched in front of you, bend one leg up and lure your dog under the crook of your knee. This works particularly well with terriers.

The time to introduce the word 'down' is just as your dog is going into the correct position. Gradually increase the amount of time before you reward him. After that, try getting him to lie down where there are minor distractions, for example in the back garden. The rule to apply is that the harder the task, the better the reward.

Never use force; this will get you into a wrestling match that you will invariably lose, or alternatively your dog will become suspicious and will immediately shy away from you.

Leave it

▶ *'Leave it' is an essential command if you want your dog to ignore an object.*

There will be many times in your dog's life when you'll want him to leave something or someone alone, such as an object he has picked up in the street, children's toys, joggers, cyclists or children playing in the park. A 'leave it' command covers all the items and people that you would rather your dog didn't touch, eat or chase. When teaching a 'leave it' command, let your dog decide what position he wants to

go in. You shouldn't suddenly ask him to obey two commands at once, for example 'leave it' followed by 'down'.

Get five or six high-value treats and put them to one side. Put a dog biscuit in the palm of your hand, show it to your dog, close your hand and hold your closed hand under his nose. Let your dog sniff, paw and lick your hand, but don't say anything. Your dog will eventually back off, confused,

but as soon as he moves his face away from your hand, say "leave it" and give him one of the treats. You're teaching him that he won't get the object you've told him to leave. At the end of the exercise, put the dog biscuit away and don't give it to him. As you teach the 'leave it' command, your dog should begin to back off faster and sit patiently, and you can then hold your hand open for a couple of seconds before you praise and reward him.

When he is consistently leaving treats in the palm of your hand, start making the exercise more difficult. Try higher-value rewards for him to leave, and roll a biscuit along the floor, being prepared to put your hand over it to begin with until he understands he has to leave it.

When he has mastered all these 'leave it' commands, put your dog on the lead and let him see you put some food away. Tether him to something or ask someone to hold him while you do this. The food should be about 3m (10ft) away from you. Walk toward it and, as soon as your dog begins to pull toward the treat, walk backward until your dog stops pulling toward the treat and looks at you. Then reward and praise him for looking at you.

Once your dog has realized that looking at you gets him a reward, it should be easier to get him closer and closer to the treat on the floor, until he will eventually walk past.

TRAINING A DOG TO LEAVE AN ITEM ALONE

1 Hold a treat in the palm of your hand under your dog's nose, then close your hand. Don't say anything.

2 Let your dog sniff, paw and lick. He will eventually back off. When he does, say "leave it" and give him the treat.

3 Next, make the exercise more difficult: put a few treats on the floor and ask your dog to "leave it".

4 If your dog sits patiently, reward him with a treat. Over time he will wait and look at you whenever you say "leave it".

Stay

▶ *Teaching your dog the 'stay' cue will help to keep him out of danger.*

The 'stay' command means 'stay where you are until I get back to you'. So, if your dog accidentally escapes out the front door and runs across a road, the wisest course of action is to tell him to stay where he is until you can get him. He'll also need to master the 'stay' command if you want him to enter dog competitions.

There are two aspects of the exercise to work on: duration and distance. Gradually increase the amount of time he stays, while you move further and further away. He needs to have the confidence to stay where he is. In fact, this is much harder for a dog than you realize, so never get angry if he can't stay for long and comes bounding up to you. After all, the training you have done with him previously has been right in front of him, with a reward just seconds away. If you do get angry, he'll get stressed, which will make him even more likely to get up and follow you. If he does break a 'stay', take him back to where he was, put him back in position and go back a few steps so that he understands what you want.

First, tell him to sit but don't move away yet. Say "stay" while holding up the flat of your hand (this visual command will reinforce the verbal cue). Then count to five and reward him. When he can sit and stay for 1 minute, you can begin to move away from him. Do this very slowly, taking one step back, then move back and reward him, adding plenty of verbal praise.

The next time you do this, take two steps back before going back to him with a reward, and so on. If he gets up to follow you when you move back, he does not understand what you want.

In that case, go back a few stages and start all over again. Continue to increase the duration and distance in small stages, making it as easy as possible for your dog to succeed.

When you are confident that your dog understands the word 'stay' and you can move a few steps away, start to train in a safe area with distractions. This could be in a quiet area of your local park. Again, gradually build up time and distance, and always praise him when he gets it right.

TRAINING A DOG TO STAY

1 Begin by teaching your dog to remain still. Say "stay" while holding up the flat of your hand.

2 Count slowly to five, and if your dog has not moved away, reward him with a small food treat.

3 When he can stay still for 1 minute by your side, begin moving away. Very slowly, take one step back.

4 Return and give him a reward, then gradually increase the number of steps. Always return and reward him.

Wait

▶ *Teaching your dog to wait will help him with patience and good manners.*

There is a subtle difference between 'stay' and 'wait' commands. 'Stay' means 'stay where you are until I get back to you' and is usually used from a safety point of view when it is essential that a dog doesn't move, for example when he might have slipped out of his lead while standing beside a busy main road. In contrast, 'wait' means 'we are going to do something else' and is more a case of good manners when you want your dog to keep quiet and behave, for example while waiting for his dinner or waiting on the lead to cross a road. You could also ask your dog to wait while you open the front door, so that he learns to leave the house in an orderly fashion, instead of barging past you in his hurry to get to the park. Similarly, asking your dog to wait while you open the car door is a good habit to get into.

TRAINING A DOG TO WAIT

1 Hold on to your dog's collar while you put a treat just out of his reach. Don't say anything at this stage.

2 Allow him to pull toward the treat while you hold his collar. When he relaxes and looks at you, say "wait".

3 Let go of his collar and allow him to go and get the treat. Praise him for having waited patiently.

4 Practise the exercise until your dog can successfully wait without you having to hold on to his collar.

To teach a dog to wait, take a small treat and hold your dog by the collar. Roll the treat away from you, just out of reach of your dog. Don't say anything to him yet, but let him pull toward the treat while you hold on to his collar. He will eventually relax, sit and possibly look at you. Say "wait" and then let him get the treat.

Next, teach him to wait at the front door. Put him on a lead, get him to sit next to you and ask him to wait. Open the front door a bit and, if he gets up to charge out, close it immediately, making sure you don't trap his nose. Drop the lead, walk away, wait a few seconds, then try again. It may take six or seven attempts before your dog sits nicely while you open the door, and don't forget to reward him on each occasion. Teaching him this self-control will make going out for a walk a much calmer experience.

When in the park, practise asking your dog to wait while on a flexi-lead or long line first – not when your dog is running, which is too dangerous. Wait until there are other dogs or people around. Let your dog get slightly ahead of you, then ask him to wait. Put the brake on the flexi-lead or hold on to the line and, when he stops to look at you, praise and reward him. Only do this when he is walking slowly; he may hurt his neck if he is running.

Eye contact

▶ *A dog should enjoy eye contact. It will improve a shy dog's confidence.*

Teaching your dog to make eye contact with you should be one of the most rewarding things you do with him. Once learned, it's a good exercise that you can use again and again, for example when you want to keep your dog's attention so that he doesn't go dashing off after a group of dogs in the park. It's also very useful if you have a shy dog. Teaching him eye contact is actually a good game to play, and will help build his confidence.

It used to be thought that you should never look a dog in the eye. However, this only applies to staring a dog down when he's wrong, in which case he'll associate eye contact with punishment. Because children are about head-height with dogs, they will almost always look dogs in the eye. If a pet has not been trained to make

eye contact, there is a risk of being bitten in the face by an apprehensive pet. By teaching a dog that eye contact is a rewarding experience, he will not fear being looked at; in fact he will positively look forward to it.

Start in a room without any distractions, holding a handful of treats, with your dog off the lead. Show him the treats, then close your hand and hold it out to the side. The dog will try to jump up to get the treats, but if you wait, he'll eventually sit down and glance at you. Tell him he's a good boy as soon as he looks you in the eye, and reward him by tossing the treat away from you to encourage him to move away. What you are hoping is that he'll come back and sit in front of you again, offering more eye contact. After about five or

six attempts, your dog should sit in front of you and look at you when you hold out your hand. When he is looking you in the eye consistently, you can begin to say "watch me" so that he understands the command.

If your dog is particularly shy, he may find it difficult to make eye contact, but persevere with the task, rewarding even a glance in your direction. Proceed at your dog's pace.

TRAINING A DOG TO MAKE EYE CONTACT

1 Begin with your dog off the lead. Show him a handful of treats, then hold them out to your side.

2 Be patient while your dog watches your hand and tries to get the treats. Eventually he will look up at you.

3 When he looks you in the eye, toss a treat away from you. After eating it, he should return for more eye contact.

Recalling your dog

Of all the commands that you will teach your dog, a recall is one of the most important. If your dog does not come back when called, he'll always have to be kept on a lead. This will reduce his social skills with other dogs and people, as he will not be free to interact. Being on the lead all the time would also mean that he couldn't have as much fun following weird and wonderful scents, snuffling away through the undergrowth.

There are many reasons why a dog does not come back when called, the most obvious being that he has never been trained. Owners can be lulled into a false sense of security when their dogs are puppies, because they rarely go off, instead tending to stay by their side. However, a dog may suddenly realize it's not so bad being away from his owner, and when you shout "come back", you might as well be yodelling in another language.

Some dog owners think that just calling a dog by his name when he's off playing with other dogs will get an instant result. It won't. Calling like this

▼ *Be enthusiastic and reward your dog keenly when he comes to you.*

means that when you use his name in future, he'll associate that with the end of his fun and the end of the walk, making him less likely to return.

So it's important when training him to come back that you use a suitable reward – one that compensates him well for being told to stop chasing other dogs. Ordinary dog biscuits will not be enough. Instead, try one of the home-made treats shown earlier in this book. With recall training it is important to put a firm foundation down before you move on to the next level. Always set your dog up for success.

The secret to getting your dog to obey is time, work and plenty of patience. Once your dog has learned to return to you, you can safely let him off the lead so that he can have some fun on his own. Training a recall is all about conditioning your dog so that when he hears the 'come' command, he will automatically turn and come charging back to you.

SIMPLE RECALL
Start teaching him in a place where there are no distractions. Carry a handful of treats and your dog's

▲ *Once your dog is trained to come to you, he'll be free to play off the lead.*

favourite toy. Feed him a few treats from your hand to get his attention, then toss a small treat away from you. If necessary, show him where it has gone and, just as he is eating it, back away a few steps from him and call his name. When he looks toward you, praise him just for looking up and paying attention. As he comes back to you, get really excited that he is coming in your direction – give him a round of applause. Dog owners can be reticent about praising their dogs, but getting a recall is a situation in which you should go overboard with praise. Make his tail wag with happiness.

When he gets back to you, give him a treat immediately and let him play with his favourite toy. Don't tell him to sit before giving him the reward; this would incorrectly reward the sit rather than the recall.

Then toss another treat out and, again, just when he has eaten the treat, call him by name. As he is coming toward you, say "come". Only do this five or six times, then finish. If you carry out short training sessions four or five times a day, your dog will stay alert and happy. You can practise recalls in the kitchen when the kettle is boiling, tossing treats up and down the room when the advertisements are on the television – in fact, during any spare couple of minutes that you have.

TRAINING A DOG TO COME BACK

1 In a place with no distractions, feed your dog some tasty treats by hand, to get his attention.

2 Toss one small treat a short distance away from you, showing him where you want him to go.

3 While your dog is busy finding and eating his food treat, walk a few steps away from him.

4 When he has finished eating, call him. Praise him for looking up. In later repetitions, say "come" at this point.

5 When he begins to run back to you, get really excited – smile, give him a round of applause and praise him.

6 As soon as he reaches you, reward him with a food treat and/or a favourite toy, then repeat the process.

◀ *Use extra-tasty treats for rewarding recalls in places with distractions.*

RECALLING WITH DISTRACTIONS

The next stage is to try this training in the garden, where there are plenty of distractions. Use a highly visible reward such as a chunk of red cheese that can be seen in the grass (this will give hunting breeds plenty of stimulation). Let your dog use his sense of smell to hunt down the treat. To create even more excitement, throw the cheese behind you when your dog is running toward you so that he has to fly past you to get the reward. This makes recall a really exciting game for your dog.

After about a week of this training, choose a time when your dog is in the garden and you are indoors, watching him through the window. Call him by name and give the cue 'come'. If he comes charging into the house, give him a really high-value reward and praise him until he wags his tail. He now understands what 'come' means.

Having achieved this result, take your training to the next level. This requires a willing volunteer, some boring dog biscuits and a handful of really tasty treats. Place your dog by the volunteer and tell them to hold an ordinary dog biscuit right under his nose. Stand about 3.6m (12ft) away, then call your dog. Repeat the command until he comes. Initially you'll have to call him five or six times but, eventually, he'll respond more quickly. Always give him a special reward so that he knows it's worth responding. Give him better treats for better responses, until you eventually give him a handful of chicken.

If you practise a little and often, you'll quickly reach this stage. The secret is to add the command 'come' after you call his name and he runs toward you. This ensures that it's second nature for him to come whenever you ask him to.

▼ *Begin recall training indoors, using a treat such as a piece of cheese.*

For the final stage, you need a volunteer who knows your dog. Stand about 12m (40ft) away from your volunteer, get them to call your dog and, as he obeys and goes off, call him back when he is halfway there. Then try calling him back from playing with a friend's dog and even from strange dogs. Never forget how good he has been to obey you – make sure he gets an excellent treat for every recall. Having a good recall is the most important command that you teach your dog. A life on the lead is not good and, with that in mind, never stop rewarding successful recalls.

WHISTLE RECALLS

There are a number of benefits to teaching your dog to respond to a whistle, not least because a whistle is much louder than your voice and can easily cut through a blasting winter wind. If you have a quiet voice and don't like shouting, a whistle is ideal.

▼ *Instead of food, playing a game is also a good reward for coming back.*

Another advantage is that the sound is always the same, whether you walk the dog yourself, use dog walkers or if different members of your family walk the dog. It is a clear, distinct sound that will cut through any distractions or the sound of people talking. It is used for one command only – 'come here' – and should not be confused with anything else.

There are many different whistles on the market, and a loud one is best. The range includes specialist gun dog whistles and a referee's whistle, and you might also like to try a silent dog whistle. It doesn't matter which one you use, provided you stick to it.

Like recall training, whistle training is all about repetition, so that the dog instinctively associates the sound with the command 'come here'. When training your dog, carry out the above procedure but exchange the 'come' command for a blow on the whistle. You can also make the association between the whistle and good news at meal times: hold a bowl of food, blow the whistle, then give your dog his dinner. If you do that for a week at every meal when he is a puppy (three times a day), he'll quickly make the connection. If your dog will retrieve a ball, try blowing the whistle as he comes toward you. This will strengthen the association between the whistle and the 'come' command. Finally, if you take your dog on a walk with a friend, practise whistle recalls between the two of you, increasing the distance as his reliability increases. Always take rewards out with you.

From a safety point of view, your dog needs a strong recall; continuing to reward him intermittently will keep the recall response strong.

TRAINING A WHISTLE RECALL

1 Throw a treat a short distance away from you, making sure your dog sees where you want him to go.

2 After your dog has found the treat and eaten it, blow a whistle. Praise him for looking at you.

3 When he comes running back to you, smile and encourage him, stroke him and give him a food treat.

4 Take the time to praise your dog, and always use very tasty treats when training a recall with distractions.

Lead-walking

▶ *Reward your dog when he obeys your command to 'walk close'.*

Teaching your dog to walk on a loose lead is one of the hardest things you'll have to do. Roads and parks are full of fascinating smells, the scents of other dogs and the aroma of dropped food, all of which entice your dog to pull away and investigate. When he becomes an adolescent, the urge to scent-mark over those smells will be very strong, and there'll be an extra need to pull you in all kinds of directions. In addition, most dogs quickly realize that if they pull when they are keen to get to the park, their owner tends to walk faster.

Most dog owners do not want obedience-style heelwork; all they want is to keep their arm in its socket and to have a pleasant walk! Dog-training classes often teach you to walk a dog on your left, simply because obedience competitions demand it, but for the average dog owner it really doesn't matter which side he walks on. If you are walking along a main road, it is usually safest to have your dog walking on the inside, away from the traffic.

Lead-walking can be difficult in terms of being consistent. If you are pushed for time and have to get home to leave for work after the morning

walk, there isn't always time to stop every time your dog pulls. If so, unfortunately your dog's pulling behaviour will be reinforced.

There are many training aids to facilitate lead-walking. If you have a strong dog, a harness is a great help, and a head collar will give you more control, provided your dog will accept wearing one over his nose. Try out a few different ones to see which type your dog is most comfortable with.

Start by training your dog to walk by your side without his lead on. If your dog cannot do this without being distracted, he will not be able to walk on a loose lead. Begin by sitting him by your side, feeding him a few treats to get his attention. Pat the side of your leg as you step off to signal where you would like him to be, then reward him after a couple of steps. In fact, you cannot reward your dog too much in the early stages of teaching him to walk on a lead. Every couple of steps, offer another reward. Eventually, however, you'll want him to learn to walk calmly by your side with his head up, taking in a wide range of sights

▼ *If your dog likes to pull hard, a harness will give you more control.*

and smells; it would be unnatural for him to trot along while fixated on your hands and a possible reward. Until he reaches this stage, reward him when he's walking by your side, but don't stop to make him sit for his reward, otherwise he'll think he's being rewarded for the act of sitting.

If your dog pulls ahead, resist the urge to yank him back on the lead – this is a sure way to damage his neck and hurt your shoulder. Instead, stop walking and take a couple of steps back until your dog is by your side. Get him to sit, gain his attention, then start again. Do not praise and reward him for just being by your side; save that for when he's walking calmly by your side on a loose lead.

Continue using vocal praise when he is positioned exactly where you want him to be, and always use the words 'walk close' when he is in the right position – not when he is pulling. Also reward him when he obeys you, especially when he stays by your side while walking past a distraction. The more encouragement you give him, the more he'll learn not to pull and try to investigate everything. When he consistently and automatically responds to your commands, you can dispense with the food treats.

TRAINING A DOG TO WALK ON A LOOSE LEAD

1 Begin by rewarding your dog for being at your side without a lead. Feed him a small treat to get his attention.

2 As you step forward, pat the side of your leg. This is to let your dog know where you want him to be.

3 When your dog stands up and walks by your side, reward him with another food treat. Repeat this every few steps.

4 Once your dog can successfully walk by your side, carry out the same training procedure with a lead.

5 Pat your leg to show your dog where you want him. Do not pull on the lead; let your dog walk forward on his own.

6 Do not reward him for sitting. Wait until he walks calmly by your side with a loose lead, then give him a treat.

Settle down

▶ *Your dog should be able to settle down quietly and happily when asked.*

Having a dog that is able to settle down means that he won't be a pest when you are trying to eat a meal, that he'll lie beside you when you have visitors, and that he'll happily curl up next to you when you are reading. In many households there's already enough noise and confusion. You don't need to add to it by having an agitated dog, and it would be a shame to have to isolate him by putting him in a crate, locking him in another room or shutting him behind a baby gate. The command 'settle down' will allow calm to reign over the chaos.

When your dog is lying down of his own accord, reward him with a small treat, tell him he's a good boy and stress the word 'settle'. The more you reward a dog's natural behaviour, the more he'll be able to do it, and

the delight of this command is that it doesn't involve one fixed position. The dog can flop over on his side, curl up, roll or stretch. He can do anything, as long as he is settled. Unfortunately we often ignore dogs (and children) when they are quiet, not realizing that such behaviour should be actively encouraged. The more you reward a particular behaviour, the more often your dog will do it.

When you teach your dog to settle, make sure he's tired, for example after an evening meal or his walk. Put him on a long, loose lead so that he can sit, lie or stand while you watch television. Ignore him, and while he may find this (and being tethered) rather odd and get restless, he will eventually settle down. Don't say anything (no 'down' or 'sit' cues); just wait him out

until he settles. The hardest part is getting him to settle down for the first time, and thereafter he should find it easier and easier. Don't go overboard with the praise, because this will just make him jump straight back up again. Gently stroke his head, slip him a treat and say "settle down". The more you practise, the easier it will get, and the longer amount of time your dog will remain settled.

TRAINING A DOG TO SETTLE DOWN

1 Choose a time when your dog is tired, such as after a meal or a walk. Put him on a long lead and sit quietly.

2 Ignore him for a while. Do not say anything; wait him out. Eventually he should lie down by your side.

3 When he settles, reward him quietly by gently stroking his head. Give him a food treat and say "settle down".

Retrieve

▶ *Repeating your retrieval training will keep your dog well exercised.*

Some dog breeds love to retrieve more than others, with collies and labradors being high up on the list. Other dogs find retrieving a pointless exercise, but although it might take them a while to be trained, it can be done. One of the advantages of training a dog to retrieve is that you don't have to take him on a long walk to get him fully exercised. If you're feeling tired but he's bursting with adrenaline, you've only got to throw a ball. It's also a great bonding exercise for both of you.

Dogs that aren't natural retrievers need short training sessions or they'll quickly get bored, and this particularly applies to puppies. Begin in a place where there are few distractions, and don't be surprised if your dog initially picks up the toy that you have thrown and runs off in the opposite direction. Whatever you do, don't run after him or he'll think you're instigating a game of chase.

The easiest way to teach a dog to retrieve is by first teaching him to pick up an object. Have some small, tasty treats and a toy. Offer him the toy, and if he takes it in his mouth, praise him wildly and offer him a treat. This will teach him to drop the object into your hand.

Pick up the toy again and play with it on the floor, get him interested in chasing it, then toss it a short distance away from you. As soon as he puts it in his mouth, praise him again and offer him a treat. He may spit the toy out and come to you for his treat, but don't worry – this is only the beginning of the game.

If your dog doesn't seem interested in picking up the toy, play a fun game of hide-and-seek with it – showing him the object, then hiding it behind your back. When you eventually get his interest, throw the toy away. If he chases it and picks it up, praise and reward him. If he really has no interest, go further back in the sequence and reward him for just sniffing the toy a couple of times.

By doing the training a little and often, and putting the toy away after each game, your dog's retrieval skills should gradually build up over a couple of sessions.

TRAINING A DOG TO RETRIEVE AN ITEM

1 Have some tasty treats handy. Offer your dog a toy, but keep it just out of his reach; this should get him excited.

2 Let him hold the toy. Put a treat under his nose. When he lets go of the toy, praise him and give him the treat.

3 Once he has learned that dropping the toy gets him a reward, toss the toy a short distance away from you.

4 Praise him for picking up the toy, and give him a treat when he brings it back to you. Do not chase him.

Drop it

There will be times when your dog picks up something he shouldn't, and teaching him to 'drop it' means you can retrieve your possessions without it becoming a battle of wills. From a safety point of view, it is important that your dog is able to give things up willingly on command.

It is best to teach this is in stages. Use a favourite toy that can be used for tug, and some very tasty treats – the smellier the better. Offer your dog the toy and initiate a game of tug. Soon after, put a treat right under his nose, at which point he should drop the toy and take the treat. He may take a couple of seconds to think about it, but bear with him. The crucial point is to say "drop it" at the moment he drops the toy. Then show him the toy again and have another game.

Play this game of tug a few times each day, always putting a treat under his nose and saying "drop it" at the appropriate moment. After a few days,

try saying "drop it" before you offer the treat and, if he drops the toy, give him a handful of treats as the jackpot.

Your dog should learn to give things up as a young puppy, and whenever you take something away from him, always swap it with something equally rewarding. Don't take bones and other prized objects away from him just because you think you should, because this is the fastest way to teach a dog to guard his possessions. If he does tend to guard bones, food or toys, get specialist help from a behaviour counsellor.

When your dog has mastered the 'drop it' command, this will open up the possibility of playing a whole range of interactive games. Most dogs love fetching a ball, but nothing can be more frustrating for an owner than having to hunt all over the house for a dropped toy. Because your dog has learned that he can exchange a toy for a treat, he will now bring the ball back

▲ *Teaching your dog to drop an object will make games of fetch fun.*

to you to gain his reward. You could also try hiding a toy and get your dog to seek it out and return it to you. These games will help to keep your dog's mind and body well exercised.

Some formal obedience tests involve retrieving and returning an item, and dogs working to the gun must seek and return fallen birds. For all these disciplines, a well-taught 'drop it' command is a very good basis on which to build.

TRAINING A DOG TO DROP AN OBJECT

1 Offer your dog one end of a tugger toy and initiate a game of tug-of-war, pulling the toy away from him.

2 Let go of the tugger and take a treat out of your pocket. Hold the treat right under his nose.

3 Allow him time to decide what to do. Say "drop it" as soon as he drops the toy, give him the treat and praise him.

Phasing out the reward

The ultimate aim of training your dog is to get him to obey your commands whether you provide a reward or not. When your dog is a puppy you need to reward and bribe him, but that state shouldn't exist forever. You can't keep stashing away rewards that will excite him (which soon becomes a practical problem), just to make sure he's obedient. The use of food becomes bad psychologically: there's a very real danger that your dog will become too reliant on rewards and bribes, and will never obey a command without food. In addition, rewards can become boring over time, and the behaviour you want to encourage will gradually diminish. But at what point should you start phasing out food treats? The answer is as soon as your dog understands a command and can respond correctly with a treat.

Put your treats somewhere that you can reach them but your puppy cannot, such as in your pocket or in a treat bag. Using the same hand movement that you used with the food lure, ask your dog to sit. When he does, praise him profusely. Repeat the request several times, sometimes giving your dog a treat when he sits and sometimes not. There may be some confusion on your puppy's part when you first dispense with the food lure, but bear with him. You may need to ask him twice to begin with.

When your puppy manages to sit successfully without the food in your hand, you can now go on to rewarding the best responses. Make the rewards intermittent, only rewarding the very best responses and ignoring those that aren't as good. Use different rewards, such as a game of tug or throwing a ball, combined with verbal praise.

Improving training is all about getting the best out of your dog, so now is the time to ask more of him. Ask your dog to follow a few commands before you praise him – maybe a 'sit' and then a 'down'. Next, ask him to sit, walk ten paces away from him, then return and praise him. Then try asking him to sit, lie down and sit again, and then reward him. Don't be too predictable with your training; ask for cues in different combinations and reward your dog at different times.

Delay the time your dog follows a cue and gets his reward. Ask him to sit, count to ten, then reward him. Next time, ask him to lie down, count to five and then give him his reward. You will get the best out of your dog if you keep him guessing. If your training is boring and predictable, he too will find it boring and predictable and you won't get the behaviour you deserve for all your hard work.

PHASING OUT FOOD REWARDS

▲ *Eventually, praise, strokes and games can replace food rewards.*

When you begin asking more of your dog, he may break his positions – he is used to being rewarded immediately, but you are changing the conditions. Don't panic; just put him back in position and try an easier task. If you were trying for a 10-second sit and your dog gets up, put him back calmly and count to five instead. In time he'll get it right, and his confidence will grow accordingly.

1 Hide some treats in a bag. Ask your dog to sit, using the hand movements you used before, but without any food.

2 When he sits, praise him. On some occasions give him a food treat; at other times, reward him with a game.

Household manners

Just as children have to be taught basic manners, so do puppies. One of the first things we teach our children is to be polite and say "please" when they want something, but we miss many opportunities to teach our dogs the same thing on a daily basis.

Using everyday life rewards is a great way to practise all the exercises that you have trained your dog to do in the context that you want him to do them. For example, if he wants to go out to the garden to go to the toilet, ask him to sit for a moment, thus training him to hold his bladder. Concentrate on life rewards such as going outdoors, walks and games, and you'll get good results.

It's best to give your dog only one cue; don't nag him. When asking him to sit before going out to the garden, if he doesn't sit the first time you ask, calmly walk away from the back door for a moment, without saying anything to him. Then go back and try again. After about the third or fourth time, he should understand.

As another example, ask your dog to sit so that you can put his lead on to go for a walk. If he begins leaping and running around in his excitement to get out the door, calmly drop the lead and walk away. After 30 seconds, go back and pick up the lead. At this stage his excitement will probably be even greater, so drop the lead again and walk away. You may want to put the kettle on and make a cup of tea when you are teaching this skill – with some dogs it will take a while before they learn that it's actually what they are doing that is responsible for your

▲ *The door is a place of excitement to your dog, so he needs good manners.*

actions. When you have the lead on and your dog is sitting calmly, put your hand on the door handle. Here, if he begins to jump around and tries to push through the door, close the door, drop the lead and walk away. Continue the process until he is able to stay calm while you're preparing for his walk.

TRAINING A DOG TO SIT CALMLY BEFORE GOING FOR A WALK

1 When it's time for a walk, pick up your dog's lead and go to the door. He may get very excited and jump up.

2 If he doesn't sit the first time you ask, drop the lead, turn around and walk away without saying anything.

3 You may have to do this a few times before he gets the message. Once he has learned to sit nicely, put his lead on.

Sitting when visitors call

▲ *It's important for your dog to learn to be calm around visitors.*

Some dogs greet visitors so enthusiastically that it can be embarrassing – or worse, your dog may cover your visitors' clean clothes with muddy paws. Most dogs jump up to get attention, so you need to avoid giving him attention such as shouting "get down", grabbing his collar to pull him away or smacking him, because even negative attention inadvertently reinforces the jumping-up behaviour.

Even if visitors tell you, "I don't mind; I love dogs", this doesn't mean your dog should be allowed to jump up on them. If he jumps up on children or on the elderly, he may knock them over, with serious consequences. Your dog will not be able to discriminate between who he can and can't jump on, so you must be consistent with all household visitors.

The secret is not to let jumping up become a habit in the first place. When your puppy jumps up on you, take a step back so that his feet land on the floor, then kneel down to his level to say hello. This means there'll be no reason for him to jump. It's important to teach children to do the same thing, because it's usually children who shout when the puppy is jumping up, which only gets the puppy more excited.

If jumping up is already an established habit, it will take a bit longer to teach your dog an alternative behaviour. You need a willing volunteer to help you. Have your dog on the lead when your volunteer calls. Ask the visitor to stand beyond the reach of your dog. Let your dog pull toward the visitor, but ignore the dog's behaviour – don't shout at him, push him into a sit position or yank him back on the lead. The idea is that you are teaching your dog the consequences of his behaviour.

When the lead has gone loose and your dog has settled down, reward him. Don't ask your visitors to reward him, however, because there is going to be a time when you'll have a guest that is not keen on dogs; you'll want your dog to sit quietly by your side when they are visiting. Conversely, if someone were to come in and provide a reward, your dog would begin to expect rewards from everyone he comes across – in the park and in the street.

Note that you don't always have to use food as a reward. Instead, you could have a quick game of tug for sitting quietly when visitors call.

TRAINING A DOG TO SIT WHEN VISITORS CALL

1 Find a willing volunteer to help you. Have your dog on a lead and ask your visitor to come into the room.

2 Allow your dog to pull toward the visitor. Do not try to stop your dog – do not shout at him or pull the lead.

3 Eventually your dog will sit down. As soon as he does, praise him and reward him with a food treat.

Distance, duration and distractions

We need our dogs to follow commands, whether they are on or off the lead, in a park full of dogs or walking along the road, and for the length of time that we require. Many owners become dismayed that their dogs follow all their commands in the house and in training classes, but as soon as they're outside it seems as if they'd never been to a training class before.

When you're ready to train your dog to obey you at a distance, it's best to keep distractions to a minimum to begin with, and increase the duration of the exercises a little at a time. Note that you will have to increase the number of rewards when you make the exercises more difficult.

Once he is performing well in your usual training environment, begin training in the park where you take your dog for a walk. The difficulty in

this is that your dog probably only associates the park with playing with other dogs, and he may be more keen to run off rather than complete your obedience exercises. But if you're patient, you will see results. Note that if you increase the value of the reward, it's a good idea to make sure any other dogs are as far away as possible.

DISTANCE

When you begin training in a park where you have never done distance exercises before, don't try a difficult 1-minute 'stay' right at the beginning of the session. Instead, ask for several short sessions of 'sit' while you walk a couple of steps away from your dog, then come straight back to him. Don't start off with long distances; it is better to make it easy for him and gradually build up his confidence. Use the

environment as a reward. For example, if he is on a long lead, you could let him walk toward a tree for a good sniff. If he pulls toward something he wants without sitting first, take a couple of steps back as a penalty, then try again. When he gets it right, use rewards that your dog enjoys. Once he can sit successfully, stay and watch, let him off the lead and continue the training.

DURATION

As well as increasing the distance between you and your dog, you can also begin to increase the amount of time between the desired behaviour and the reward. This training works best when you're unpredictable. For example, vary the length of time that you stand back from your dog during a 'stay' command. On the first occasion,

WORKING WITH DISTANCE, DURATION AND DISTRACTIONS

1 When training your dog to 'stay' while outdoors, gradually increase the distance between you and your dog.

2 Also try increasing the duration of time between your dog's desirable behaviour and the reward.

3 Finally, add distractions to your training. For example, ask your dog to sit, then make a phone call.

CHECKING THAT A DOG UNDERSTANDS A CUE

1 To test if your dog understands 'walk close', take his lead off in the garden. Say his name to get his attention.

2 Take a few steps back and say "walk close". If your dog understands, he will make eye contact and approach.

3 When he walks by your side, reward him with a handful of food treats and praise him enthusiastically.

reward him after 25 seconds, the next time 5 seconds, then 10 seconds. Similarly, when teaching him to walk on a lead, reward him after a couple of steps, then 10, 5 and 20 steps. This will keep your dog guessing and, more importantly, it will make him try harder to get you to reward him.

DISTRACTIONS

It's important to hold training sessions not just in classes but in the real world, which is packed with distractions, because that's where your dog needs to obey you. Make sure he can walk on a loose lead without pulling forward when he sees a family member approaching. You don't want him dashing across a road and causing an accident. Can he leave a toy on the floor when he walks past it, and sit while you talk on the telephone? Adding distractions is challenging, but make sure that whenever you increase the pressure to follow commands, you always initially increase the reward.

DOES YOUR DOG UNDERSTAND?

When you take your training 'out on the road', you will soon find out if it has worked. Does your dog really understand that 'sit' means 'sit', wherever you are, in different environments and with distractions? Similarly, does he understand that 'walk close' means he needs to keep close to your leg whether he is on or off the lead? Most dogs learn to walk on a loose lead because we use the lead to control where they are – they know they are tethered to us, but do not necessarily understand the command. However, if your dog is off the lead and you need him by your side, understanding the cue is important so that he can come quickly and walk with you.

Test your dog out in the garden, when he is not distracted. Start walking, then say your dog's name followed by the cue 'walk close' (or whatever cue you use). If he comes and walks by your side, give him a handful of treats.

The secret to teaching him the cue properly is to name the behaviour at the exact time he is doing it. For example, say "sit" just as his bottom hits the floor, not before or after. This will make him associate the action with the cue. If you get it exactly right, he will sit the first time you ask. Training is a two-way process: you have to learn his language and he has to learn yours. You must teach him which actions match the sounds you make.

▼ *Your dog should still listen to you even when there are other distractions.*

Essential training reminders

To help you remember the key points when training your dog to follow basic commands, here is a quick summary.

TRAIN RIGHT AWAY

The more a dog behaves in a certain way, the more ingrained this behaviour becomes. This applies to both acceptable and unacceptable behaviours. So, it's your responsibility to start training your puppy as soon as you can after the age of 12 weeks, to make sure he's behaving the way you want him to, and doesn't completely disrupt your life.

HAVE A PLAN

Avoid the temptation to be exclusively negative, and don't fixate on what you don't want your dog to do. Decide what you would like him to do. Have a series of goals. Imagine him in, say, three years' time. How would you like him to behave then? Make sure you teach him what's required.

STAY CALM

It's unfair to both you and your dog to undertake training when either of you is angry, grumpy, stressed or just not in the mood. It's far better to wait until you're both happy, alert and responsive, which will give

◀ Use a variety of rewards, particularly your dog's favourite toy.

your dog a much better chance of learning his lessons. If you do train him when you're in a bad mood, he may well pick up your stress, and you're more likely to snap and be over-critical when what he really needs is encouragement and kindness.

BE CONSISTENT

It's all too easy to confuse a dog by using the same words to mean different things. For example, the word 'down' is often used in very different contexts: when your dog is jumping up on a person; when you want him to get off the sofa; when you want him to lie down; and when he is snuffling scraps on the breakfast table. It is no surprise that your dog might look confused or completely ignore you. For this reason, it's important to make sure the whole family uses the same set of commands.

◀ Stay calm and consistently praise and reward your puppy whenever he does something good.

▶ Be relaxed in your training and your dog will respond better. It is best to train when you're in a good mood.

LEARN BODY LANGUAGE

If you can read your dog's body language, you'll be able to help him out of situations when he's not coping. For example, understanding that a dog's yawn is actually a stress signal – not a sign that he's tired or bored with training – means that you need to put more effort into helping him, instead of giving up because you think he's had enough.

TELL HIM HE'S A GOOD BOY

As with children, it's very easy to focus on bad behaviour and ignore the good, taking the latter for granted.

◄ *Crates keep your dog safe and are also a good aid for house-training.*

USE CRATES

When used correctly, the crate is a brilliant idea. It's a place the dog can call his own, and where you can safely put him when he's going through the chewing phase and can't be supervised. It also makes a good holding pen if you are having a children's party and don't want him jumping up, giving nips and bites, with the children getting him overexcited. If you take your dog on holiday, let him sleep in a crate so that he has to whine to wake you up when he wants to go to the toilet. If he does have an accident in it, he won't stain the carpet.

REMEMBER, HE IS JUST A DOG

All the behaviour that your dog displays is dog behaviour. Don't forget it. We may not live comfortably with biting, barking, digging and fighting, but remember that they are all perfectly natural to him. What we can do is influence a dog's basic behaviour, and make it more acceptable. Don't leave

▲ *Training will often reap its own rewards.*

things to chance; dogs have to be trained. If you sometimes think he is being naughty, try making a list of what you did as a child, and as an adult. Who was worse?

ABOVE ALL, HAVE FUN

Training shouldn't be stressful. It needs to be relaxed and fun. The happier and more confident your dog is, the quicker he'll respond to your commands. So if the training is going wrong, take a rest and have a rethink. What are you doing wrong?

▼ *Training should involve all the family, and it should be fun.*

But don't do it. To reinforce your dog's behaviour when he's being good, go out of your way to praise him. Conversely, ignore him when he's bad. He'll feel deprived when he isn't being regularly praised, and will soon learn that good behaviour is worth learning because it brings happiness, games and treats. Remember to tell him he's a good boy just for lying quietly beside you, and give him a stroke when he sits at your side while you're having a conversation. The more you reward such behaviour, the more often your dog will display it.

CARRY TREATS IN YOUR POCKET

You never know when you will have a chance to reinforce your dog's good behaviour, so always carry treats.

MANAGE THE ENVIRONMENT

If your dog raids the bin, steals food off the worktop or jumps up on visitors, manage the environment until you can train him otherwise. Put the bin out of reach, put food away and put him in the kitchen with some treats when visitors arrive. Also teach your children to keep their toys tidy so that he can't run away with them. If he pulls when on the lead, use a head collar or harness. By managing the environment, you'll reduce tension between you and your dog.

HOW TO SOLVE COMMON PROBLEMS

There will be many times during the first few months of owning a puppy that you might wonder if you have taken on more than you can cope with. Biting, chewing, digging, stealing and attention-seeking behaviour can stretch your patience to the limit. Some behaviours that puppies engage in are specific to their breed. For example, nipping children's ankles is common with the herding breeds (the collies and shepherds); digging can be a speciality of the terriers; and retrievers like carrying things. Such genetic behaviour can never be eradicated completely, but it can be redirected in a more useful way. Everybody would like a perfect dog, but these do not come ready-made. As soon as possible, owners need to identify behaviour that could lead to problems. With kindness, understanding and consistency, and occasionally the help of experts, most can be solved.

◀ *Puppies will play with anything that is left around, such as electric cables, mobile phones and shoes. You can minimize this by providing chew toys.*

Biting

Like a baby, a puppy explores texture and taste by taking objects into its mouth and biting on them. However, a puppy learns naturally from a very young age that his teeth can hurt, and that his biting behaviour has negative consequences. For example, when he begins hurting his mother while suckling, she will get up and walk away, thus initiating weaning him on to solid food. He also learns that his siblings have teeth that can hurt, usually ending in a fight or one puppy refusing to play after a particularly painful nip.

Unfortunately, a puppy can be persistent in his biting, and if he bites children, their cries and squeals could send him into a biting frenzy. The more noise, the more biting; and the more you push the dog away, the more he throws himself back at you. Such puppies are usually overstimulated or over-tired, or terriers, and the best way to respond is by calmly getting up and ending the

▶ *Biting is natural puppy behaviour, but rough games should be discouraged.*

game. If the puppy comes after you to bite your trouser leg, then put him behind a baby gate for a 'time out' period, and you will usually find that he lies down and falls asleep. If you respond with your own freneticism, you'll simply encourage more of the same. Don't forget that dogs only have one form of defence when it comes to self-preservation, and that is their teeth. This does not make them bad – they're just being dogs.

To help your puppy learn to have a 'soft mouth', and ultimately never to use his teeth at all on human skin, you have to act like his litter mate. If you receive a painful nip from your puppy, give a high-pitched squeal and turn your back on him. He should back off,

possibly returning to lick you. Also make sure that you give him plenty of acceptable items to chew, including raggers, rawhide chews and cardboard tubes from kitchen rolls.

However, note that this method becomes less effective as your puppy grows up. An older animal is more likely to come at you with renewed vigour when you squeal. To avoid this, finish the game, get up and move away. If your dog persistently follows you, again put him calmly behind a baby gate. It is important that everyone in the house responds in the same way, discouraging all rough games. Also, don't forget that children should be supervised at all times when playing with a puppy.

TRAINING A PUPPY NOT TO BITE

1 Puppies tend to bite anything that moves and catches their attention, including trouser legs and skirts.

2 When your puppy bites your leg or clothing, turn your back on him, ignore him and walk away.

3 If you can't ignore him, give him something he is allowed to bite, such as a rawhide chew.

Chewing

An activity that all puppies and adolescent dogs enjoy, chewing usually begins during the teething stages: 4 months old for puppies, and about 8 months old for adolescents. During the teething phase, puppies explore absolutely everything with their mouths; it's their main tool when investigating the world. It's up to you to teach your puppy which objects are acceptable for him to chew, and which are not.

To a dog, all of your possessions can seem like a steady stream of chew toys. Some items are obviously dangerous, such as electric and telephone cables, television remote controls, mobile phones and poisonous plants (including many bulbs, which dogs can easily dig up). Discarded shoes and clothing can be very tempting for your dog, as can children's toys. Maybe this is a good time to train everyone in your household to put their belongings away! You should also check that

▶ *Chewing is normal when teething. Provide your puppy with a good selection of chew toys.*

cupboard doors – especially kitchen units – close correctly, so that items can be put out of harm's way.

You can never eradicate your puppy's natural need to chew, but you can make sure that he chews safely. Good pet shops sell many types of virtually indestructible chew toys, while butchers can provide raw beef shin bones. Note that you should never give your puppy chicken, pork or lamb bones. These splinter easily and the shards of bone, once swallowed, could damage the stomach and intestine, resulting in the need for veterinary treatment. Similarly, you should never give your dog plastic toys. These are dangerous because they can easily be broken into small

pieces that get stuck in a dog's throat or stomach, sometimes causing tearing and bleeding when the dog passes a stool.

Have a good look around the house and see what your puppy might be tempted by, and put all inappropriate items away. Provide him with a good selection of safe chew toys and hide chews. Ensure that all toys, either for play or chewing, are large enough so that your puppy cannot swallow them.

When teething, a knotted tea towel soaked in water and frozen will ease your puppy's sore gums. Some pet shops stock puppy teething toys that can be either frozen or chilled in the refrigerator. These are clean, dry and safe to use, even on a carpeted floor.

TRAINING A PUPPY NOT TO CHEW ITEMS

1 Keep clutter such as electric cables, mobile phones, remote controls and plants out of your puppy's reach.

2 Have a good selection of chew toys available, offering your puppy alternative, safe objects to play with.

3 Cold toys – such as an old tea towel with knots tied in it, soaked in water and frozen – will ease painful gums.

Digging

Does your garden look like the archaeologists have just left? Do you have large craters on the lawn? Are your flowerbeds shredded? You have a puppy! Most dogs will do some digging at some time, whether they're burying a toy or just for the fun of it.

The best way to control this tendency is not by trying to eradicate it, but by fencing it off – literally. Trellis off part of the garden so that there is a clearly defined area where your dog can dig. Hide a few of his favourite toys or biscuits under the soil. Teach him that this is his special digging place by allowing him to dig them up, and let him enjoy himself in his special area.

If he is digging in another part of the garden, don't chase him away or you will simply teach him a new game – next time he wants to play, he'll start digging so that you come running after him. If you don't want him to dig in any part of the garden, buy him a child's sandpit, fill it with builder's

▶ *Digging is second nature to a dog, so he needs a special area of his own in the garden. Make sure he is never left alone for long periods of time.*

sand and bury his toys or some biscuits in it. Cover the sandpit at night so that the neighbourhood cats don't use it as a toilet.

Some dogs will try to dig under the garden fence in an attempt to escape. This will be very dangerous if they succeed, so immediate action must be taken. Placing large rocks or boulders in the area where your dog is digging will put him off, but he may just move his tunnelling activities to another part of the boundary. In the short term, the best course of action is to fix strong wire mesh to the bottom of the fence

and to bury it at least 60cm (2ft) under the ground. Ensure that there are no sharp edges to the fencing so that your dog will not hurt his paws.

In the long term, try to work out why your dog feels the need to escape. Does he have enough exercise, or could he be bored? Is there anything in the garden that he is afraid of? Watch him for a period of time and see if you can work out the reason. Increasing exercise, providing mental stimulation and ensuring he is not left alone for long periods will go a long way toward solving this problem.

TRAINING A DOG TO DIG IN A SPECIAL AREA

1 Fence off a small part of the garden where it is acceptable for your dog to dig. This can be achieved with a trellis.

2 While your dog watches, bury a few toys and/or biscuits in the special fenced-off part of the garden.

3 Encourage your dog to dig in the special area, and praise him when he finds his buried treasure.

Jumping up

Particularly if you have a large breed of dog, jumping up can be a serious problem. It can be downright dangerous when a dog jumps up on children or the elderly, and although smaller dogs are not as dangerous, they can certainly be a nuisance with a prodigious spring and muddy paws. The problem is that when puppies are young, we inadvertently teach them to jump up to say hello so that we don't have to bend down to reach them. But a puppy's growth rate is so fast that within 3 months you will already have created a problem.

Training your dog not to jump up at people is extremely important, as this problem can have very serious consequences. A stranger may mistake your dog's over-enthusiastic greeting for an attack and be very frightened. This could result in an official complaint against your dog, and pleading a lack of training is not a very good defence! It's always your responsibility to control your dog.

To convert jumping up to sitting down for a greeting, ask your friends and family to help. Put your puppy on a lead and ask someone to approach him, but they must stop as soon as your dog strains on the lead to jump up. Ignore your puppy until he calms down, then reward him with a treat and get your friend to back off and approach again. It should only take four or five attempts to get your dog to understand that sitting for a greeting is the acceptable way to act. Practise on all family members, especially children. You, the owner, should always be the one to reward the dog, otherwise he will assume that everyone carries treats around, making his jumping-up behaviour even worse.

If your dog jumps up on you at other times – not just when you have visitors or when you open the front door – this is probably attention-seeking behaviour. If so, you need to walk away from him as soon as the unwanted behaviour begins.

▲ *Jumping up is a nuisance and can become a dangerous habit.*

It may take time and patience to re-model the jumping-up behaviour, but you must persevere. Your dog may have been allowed to jump up as a way of greeting for a considerable part of his life. If so, this has become a habit. He may remember how he was rewarded for this action with affection and praise when he was a puppy.

TRAINING A DOG NOT TO JUMP UP

1 Get a willing volunteer to help you. Ask them to approach your dog while you have him on a lead.

2 Ask your volunteer to stand just out of reach so that when your dog jumps up, he is unsuccessful.

3 When your dog sits, reward him with a small food treat while your volunteer remains where they are.

Barking

It is natural for dogs to bark, but persistent barking can be a big problem, bringing trouble from neighbours and the authorities. If your dog barks when left alone, there could be several reasons for this. He could be bored, he could be guarding his home, or he might be suffering from separation anxiety. Puppies often feel anxious when their owners go out, and rescue dogs in particular can suffer from separation anxiety when they are left alone – and when anxious, they bark. But it's possible to overcome the problem.

First, you need to find out what the problem is. Perhaps your dog is being left alone for too long without adequate exercise and a chance to go to the toilet (dogs hate going inside

▶ *Barking is always a nuisance, but once you have determined its cause, it can be controlled.*

the house). If this is the case, employ a dog walker. Also try taking your dog for a walk before you go to work, and leave him a good selection of toys to play with while you're out. If he barks when people walk past the window, close the door to that room so that he so that he can't see out. It may be that your dog is alarm-barking because he can hear your next-door neighbours or noise from outside the home. If you think this is the case, try leaving a

radio on when you go out. This will help to muffle any noise and make your dog feel more secure, so that he is less likely to feel he has to be on guard duty. Some dogs will also bark at cats or birds in the garden, in which case closing the curtains may help.

It is up to you to find out why your dog is barking – observe what is happening when he barks, make a checklist and then do something to change the situation.

TRAINING A DOG NOT TO BARK

1 Dogs can start to bark when you leave the house, and may suffer from separation anxiety when left alone.

2 Before you go out, leave a selection of toys with your dog to keep him occupied while he is on his own.

3 If your dog needs to be left alone for a long time, employ a dog walker to take him out for some exercise.

Stealing items

In the wild, dogs need to be opportunists, so if they see something they want, they will invariably try to take it, even if it involves fighting. This is part of the principle of 'survival of the fittest', and ensures that they have enough for their needs. Although it is a natural instinct, it is not one that we want occurring in our homes. Fortunately, wild dog behaviour has changed somewhat since dogs have become domesticated. Modern pets no longer have such a strong need to possess, and the reason for stealing has also changed slightly.

A domestic dog steals for one very good reason – to get attention. The first time he did it, his owner might've yelled, got up and ran after him, trying to get the stolen item back. Far from

▶ *Dogs steal items because they enjoy the consequence of being chased. Train them to 'leave it'.*

being a negative consequence, as far as the dog was concerned, he'd simply asked for attention and been rewarded with a good game of chase. So what does he do? Pick up another object and wait for his owner to come running.

To teach your dog not to take items, you need to ignore his stealing behaviour. However, if he takes something you can't ignore, use the commands 'leave it' or 'drop it'. If he doesn't respond, distract him by

ringing the doorbell. He should gallop away to see who has arrived at the door. Alternatively, scatter some treats over the floor. He should drop the stolen item in favour of the treats. Never chase your dog into a corner, though. This may scare him and cause him to growl, and you will have taught him that whenever he acquires something, he needs to guard it. By ensuring he has plenty of his own toys, he is less likely steal your possessions.

TRAINING A DOG NOT TO STEAL ITEMS

1 Do not ignore your dog if he takes something important that you really need, such as a tea towel.

2 Scatter some small treats on the floor to distract him, and ask your dog to 'leave it' or 'drop it'.

3 Praise your dog when he picks up the treats, and then retrieve your important possession.

Stealing food and begging at the table

Understandably, dogs can be a nuisance when there's food about. Some dog owners advocate the use of punishment and setting up booby traps, but the reward of food is usually so good that most dogs are prepared to take the risk. It's actually very simple to stop a dog from stealing food: never leave it unattended where your dog can reach it.

Similarly, if raiding the bin is becoming a nightmare, keep it out of reach. As much as anything else, this is important for health reasons. There may well be dangerous items in the rubbish bin, such as broken glass, empty cans or sharp chicken bones, which can cause your dog a bad injury, or even poisonous items. Don't risk it. Some dogs are very clever and can open refrigerator doors. Remedy this by fitting a child-proof catch.

It is also important that you are not taken in by those imploring, pleading, 'feed-me' eyes when your dog is looking up at you while you're eating at the table. If you give in and feed him a juicy sausage, he'll begin a lifetime of hoping that you'll do it again next time. Eventually the pleading will become more animated, and he will begin to paw at you, whine and bark at every mealtime.

Be aware that dogs are very good at manipulating young children and are more than happy to act as dustbins for any food the child dislikes. It does not take long for a dog to learn to steal from a small child, whether the child wants to feed the dog or not. So it is important that children, too, understand the reasons why their pet should never be fed at the dinner table.

▲ *A begging dog can become a problem and should not be indulged.*

If you do want to give your dog a treat, take some food out of his own bowl. While you are eating, keep him happy by giving him a hide chew on his bed or in his crate.

TRAINING A DOG NOT TO STEAL FOOD OR BEG AT THE TABLE

1 Keep worktops free of food, putting tempting items out of sight and making sure kitchen surfaces are kept clean.

2 Put the rubbish bin out of your dog's reach, for example into a cupboard under the sink, where he can't see it.

3 When you are eating, put a hide chew in your dog's bed or crate. This will keep him busy during mealtimes.

Jumping on the sofa

You might never want your dog to jump on the sofa, you might want to move him out the way when you sit down because he takes up so much room, or you might not want him leaving muddy marks on the furniture. What can you do? What you mustn't do is react with haste, grabbing your dog by the collar and yanking him off the sofa, accompanied by shouting at him. The next time that happens, he'll growl at you, which will only make the situation worse.

The best way to get your dog off the sofa is by using a training game, first teaching him to get on – yes, ON – the sofa. With a handful of treats, encourage him to jump on the sofa. You may want to cover the surface with an old sheet first. Reward him when he jumps up, then hold a treat near the floor to encourage him to jump off. Just as he

▶ To train your dog to stay off the sofa, you must first teach him to jump on the sofa. Having achieved this, reward him for jumping off.

is getting down, say "off" (this is preferable to "down", which can be confused with "lie down"). Go through the process several times. Once your dog has learned the command, you should be able to get him to jump down whenever you want him off the sofa.

If you let your dog into the bedroom, you can use the same 'off' command to teach him to get off the bed. The 'jump up' command can also be used to train him to jump into the car.

As mentioned, some dogs can growl when asked to get off the sofa or bed. This is usually a learned response: the first time the owner wanted to get their dog down they may have yanked him off by the collar and hurt him. If this is the case, the next time the dog is asked, he may become defensive and give a warning growl. Further, the dog may have an ear infection, in which case grabbing the collar will also hurt him.

TRAINING A DOG NOT TO JUMP ON THE SOFA

1 To teach your dog 'on' and 'off', first offer him a treat while encouraging him to jump up to retrieve it.

2 Lure your dog on to the sofa and give the cue 'on' (or 'up'). Reward him when he jumps up and eats the treat.

3 Hold a treat near the floor to lure your dog off. Give the cue 'off' and reward your dog when he jumps down.

Attention-seeking behaviour

Dogs have a large repertoire of attention-seeking behaviour, such as barking, stealing items, pawing, nudging, tail-chasing, light-chasing, chewing, jumping up, dropping toys on your lap and mounting your leg. Such behaviour is best ignored, but this is not always possible. In the case of mounting, for example, nothing tends to get attention more quickly than a dog trying to mount a child or a visitor's leg.

There is a wide variety of reasons why dogs resort to attention-seeking actions. It is always worth trying to address the possible causes as well as correcting the unwanted behaviour. Is it possible your dog has been left alone for too long or has he not had sufficient exercise? If so, increase the length and frequency of walks. See if you can make some lifestyle adjustments so that he is not left alone as much. Do you think your dog is bored or lacks mental stimulation? If so, how about taking him to obedience or agility training classes?

Also try providing him with some reward-based puzzle toys. A lot can be done to make your dog's environment more satisfying and rewarding, thus decreasing attention-seeking behaviour.

You need to think carefully about the response you give when your dog is looking for attention. For example, if you shout at him when you are trying to speak on the phone, you're actually giving him the attention he is seeking. Further, running around after him when he steals a tea towel is also giving him an attention reward.

The way to change the behaviour is to make sure you don't give him what he wants – your attention. As soon as he starts pestering you, get up quickly and walk out the room, closing the door between you and your dog. Don't stay out for long – 1 minute is enough – then go back in. At this point he will probably try even harder to get your attention. Get up and walk out the room again. If you are consistent, the problem should be eliminated within 5 days.

▲ *Dogs often demand attention when you are busy doing something else.*

It's important to involve the whole family in the training, because your dog will experiment with each family member to see which one will give him the attention he wants. Throughout the process, don't forget to reward your dog when he is doing what you do want, such as lying quietly by your side.

DEALING WITH ATTENTION-SEEKING BEHAVIOUR

1 When you are sitting on the sofa, your dog may pester you for attention by bringing you a toy and jumping up.

2 If he does this, ignore his behaviour, get up and walk away from him. Do not give him the attention he is seeking.

3 At a later time, reward your dog for good, calm behaviour. Stroke him when he lies down quietly on the floor.

Problem behaviour in the older dog

If you have an older dog displaying problems that have not been covered in this book, it is best to get specialist help. In particular, aggression toward people or other dogs really needs professional help. Other problems might have an underlying medical cause that can be picked up by a vet or qualified behaviour counsellor.

Think about your dog's genetic history, training, diet and the circumstances that provoke or are associated with his bad behaviour. Keep an eye on him and keep a diary, noting down what he does, when, for how long, and what external factors might have been the cause, then consult a vet. If you try to guess why problems occur and attempt to cure them yourself in a haphazard way, you might actually exacerbate the bad behaviour, with the dog eventually ending up in a rescue centre.

If you need specialist help, don't be afraid to seek it. Ask your vet or friends to recommend a good dog trainer and/or behaviour counsellor.

▶ *Older dogs may have problems that can take a long time to diagnose and sort out. Do not be afraid to seek specialist help from a professional, especially when dealing with aggression toward people or other dogs.*

If your vet refers you directly to a behaviourist, it is worth looking at the small print in your insurance documents to see whether you are covered for this and could make a claim. Specialist help can be costly, but it is well worth the expense if a satisfactory outcome can be achieved.

Take the diary that you have written regarding your dog's behaviour when you have your first appointment with your chosen trainer/behaviourist, as it will help them to get a clear picture of the problem. They will be able to advise you of any changes that you should make in your dog's lifestyle and help you put a remedial training programme in place. Do not expect an instant fix, but with patience and consistency most issues can usually be dealt with or, at the very least, the severity of the problem lessened.

SEEKING SPECIALIST HELP FOR AGGRESSION

1 Aggressive behaviour toward people or other dogs is not acceptable, and may require specialist help.

2 A good trainer will observe your dog and help you understand why the aggressive behaviour is happening.

3 Once the cause is understood, the trainer will then help you to manage your dog's unwanted aggression.

Index

adolescent dogs 31, 58–9, 87
aggression 17, 20, 23, 95
agility training 11
attention-seeking behaviour 35, 85, 94
barking 32, 35, 90, 94
begging 92
bitches 16, 17, 59
biting 46, 47, 85, 86
body language 30–1, 32–3, 50, 82
boredom 18, 32, 33, 37, 75, 82, 88, 90, 94
breeding 16–17, 59
breeds 18–19
 Alaskan malamutes 18
 bassett hounds 18
 beagles 18
 boxers 17, 30
 cavalier spaniels 17
 collies 11, 17, 18, 23, 31, 33, 53, 61, 85
 dalmations 17
 dobermans 30
 Fila Brasileiros 10
 German shepherds 19
 golden retrievers 17
 greyhounds 19
 guard dogs 19
 gun dogs 23, 71
 herding dogs 18, 19, 53, 85
 hound dogs 18
 hunting dogs 18, 70
 huskies 18, 30
 Japanese tosas 10
 labradors 17, 33, 61
 lurchers 18
 Northern Inuits 18
 pit bulls 10
 pointers 33
 police dogs 23
 retrievers 22, 75, 85
 rotweillers 30
 search-and-rescue dogs 23

shepherds 18, 23, 53, 85
sight hounds 18, 61
sniffer dogs 23
spaniels 18, 19, 30
St Bernards 19
terriers 7, 19, 30, 61, 85
Tibetan terriers 17
toy dogs 19
toy poodles 19
whippets 18
cars 12, 16, 21, 33, 93
chewing 58, 85, 87, 94
children 14–15, 34, 42–3, 48–9, 52, 53, 67, 83, 85, 86, 87, 92
clicker training 38–9
clipping claws 47
commands 60–83
 'come' 57, 68–9
 'down' 7, 63, 82, 93
 'drop it' 52, 76, 91
 'leave it' 7, 52, 64, 91
 'lie down' 51, 63, 93
 'off' 93
 'on' 93
 'settle down' 7, 74
 'sit' 7, 38, 51, 61, 62, 78, 79, 80, 81
 'stay' 7, 65, 80
 'time out' 35, 86
 'up' 93
 'wait' 7, 66
 'walk close' 72, 81
 'watch me' 67
costs 9 10
diet 10, 23, 24–5, 95
digging 88
distractions 57, 70, 80–1
equipment 9, 20–2
 bedding 21, 92
 brushes 22
 chew toys 43, 58, 85, 87
 clickers 22, 38–9
 combs 22
 crates 21, 34, 43, 83, 92
 flat collars 20
 food bowls 22, 49
 harnesses 20–1, 72, 83
 head collars 20, 83
 house lines 35
 identification discs 10, 20
 leads 13, 21, 66, 72–3, 83
 muzzles 12, 20

raggers 52–3
toys 7, 22, 37, 43, 52–3, 58, 82, 87, 90, 91, 94
treat bags 22
tuggers 22, 76
waste bags 22
water bowls 22
whistles 22, 71
exercise 6, 11, 23, 75, 88, 90, 94
eye contact 67
faeces 11, 13, 14, 15, 23, 45
fighting 6, 21, 58, 59, 83, 86, 91
food 9, 23, 24–5
 begging for 92
 dog chews 25, 92
 garlic 27, 36
 treats 25, 26–7, 36–7, 47, 51, 77, 83, 88, 92
genes 19, 85, 95
grooming 10, 22, 46–7
habituation 48–9
hackles 32
handling 46–7
health
 checks 49, 50
 risks 15
hips 17
household manners 78
house-training 17, 21, 43, 44–5
intelligence 19
jumping on the sofa 93
jumping up 89, 94
lead-walking 72–3
legal considerations 10, 13, 20
licences 20
lifestyle 9, 11
litters 16, 17
livestock 12, 13, 49
 cattle 12, 13
 deer 13
 horses 49
 pigs 13
 poultry 12
 sheep 12, 13
micro-chips 20
mounting legs 59, 94
names 56–7, 81
natural behaviour 19, 86, 90, 91

neutering 16
obedience training 11, 72, 76, 94
older dogs 95
personality 16
phasing out the reward 77
playing 13, 15, 52–3
 games 57, 76
 tug-of-war 52–3, 76
pregnancy 16
 phantom 16, 59
problems 84–95
punishment 33, 34–5
puppies 6, 16, 17, 21, 23, 42–3, 48–9, 50–1, 52–3, 54–5, 56–7, 86, 87, 93
puppy
 classes 9, 50–1
 parties 50–1
 -proofing 42
rabies 10
raiding the bin 34, 83, 92
recalling your dog 68–71
 whistle recalls 70–1
responsibilities 11, 12, 89
retrieval 75
rewards 7, 19, 36–7, 44, 55, 82
ringing a bell 45
safety 15, 76, 85, 87, 89, 92
scent-marking 16, 59
shyness 23, 53, 54–5, 67
socializing 6, 12, 17, 33, 48–9, 54–5, 58
spaying 16, 59
specialist help 95
stealing
 food 92
 items 91, 94
stress 33
tail-wagging 31, 68, 70
temperament 17
training classes 10
urban environment 6, 49
vaccinations 9, 10, 50
vets 16, 22, 46, 50–1
visitors 22, 79
waste bags 11
water 22, 24, 25
whistle recalls 70–1
wildlife 12, 49
worming 15, 17
yawning 32, 33

ACKNOWLEDGEMENTS

Photographers Robert and Justine Pickett would like to thank everyone who has helped them, including Rosie Pilbeam, Libby Norman and Patsy Parry.

The publisher would like to thank the following for acting as models and supplying dogs for photography: Jackie Aldis; Julie and Paige Allen; Samantha Appleby; Nikki Barrett; Reece Bridger; Lisa Bright; Deborah Cambell; Miranda Cornwall; Kirsty Cowie; Mr E. Crowdy; Loraine Day; Claire Dennis; Karen Fenwick; Anthony, Alison, Emma and Lucy Garrett; Keeley Harrison; Gemma and Megan Holdaway; Bob Humfrey; Laurence Irvine; Claire John; Emma Mather; Roy and Jill Matthews; Sam McIntyre; Koray Mustata; Libby, Ethan and Zak Norman; Matthew Nye; Tom Parham; Robert and Justine Pickett; Rosie Pilbeam; Russell and Debbie Pitman; Pip Ramel; David Shepherd; Max Spencer; Lewis Stephenson; Emily Stretton; Sally Tobutt; Jo and Louie Uffendell; Julie Watt; Alice Willett; Janette and Debra Wilson.

Thank you also to Patsy Parry, Robert and Justine Pickett and Lisa Owen for kindly allowing photography to take place at their property.

The publisher would like to thank the following for allowing their photographs to be reproduced in the book (t=top, b=bottom, l=left, r=right): Felicity Forster: 96; Lucy Doncaster: 32tl, 48b, 82t; iStockphoto: 11b, 13t, 18t, 18br, 19t, 19br, 32tr, 32b, 33t, 42t, 95t.